# JOB INTERVIEW PREPARATION AND CONVERSATION SKILLS

2-in-1 Book

Learn How to Crush Your Next Job Interview and Develop A Magnetic Charisma to Enhance Your Communication Skills

# JOB INTERVIEW PREPARATION

*Proven Techniques To Get Any Job You Want. Simple, Fast And Efficient Ways To Stand Out From The Crowd + The Top Winning Answers To The Toughest Interview Questions*

# Table of Contents

Introduction ............................................................................. 7
**Chapter 1—Score the Interview** ................................................ 11
    How to Land More Job Interviews Immediately. ...................... 11
    Tips for Building a Resume that Can Get You Hired. ............... 15
    Cover Letters: Why You Need One and How to Make Yours Irresistible. ............................................................................ 18
**Chapter 2—Dress to Conquer** .................................................. 23
    What to Wear if You're a Man. ............................................... 23
    What to Wear if You're a Woman. .......................................... 26
    Six Things You Should Not Wear to an Interview. ................... 28
    The Truth About Tattoos and Piercings. ................................. 30
**Chapter 3—Prepare Like a Boss** ............................................... 35
    How to Overcome Anxiety and Nervousness. ......................... 35
    Nine Things You Need to Research for Your Interview. ........... 39
    Other Vital Ways to Prepare for Your Job Interview. ............... 45
**Chapter 4—Questions and Answers** ........................................ 49
    12 Common Interview Questions and How to Ace Them. ....... 49
    Navigating Difficult Questions Like a Champion. .................... 55
**Chapter 5—Make a Great First Impression** .............................. 61
    Eight Things You Must Do to Make a Killer First Impression. .... 61
    How to Instantly Stand Out Among Other Candidates. .......... 65
    Confident Body Language that Puts You Ahead of the Game. ... 68
**Chapter 6—Pass with Flying Colors** ......................................... 71
    11 Things Your Prospective Employer Wants to Hear. ............ 71
    Eight Things You Won't Want to Say in a Job Interview. .......... 73
    10 Soft Skills and How to Demonstrate Them. ....................... 74

**Chapter 7—Finishing Touches ........................................................... 79**
  11 Great Questions to Ask the Hiring Manager. ......................... 79
  An Essential Guide to Salary Negotiations. ................................. 82
  What to Do When You Get a Question that Throws You Off-Guard. ............................................................................................. 86
  Is It OK to Lie?; When Is It OK to Lie in an Interview? ............. 87

**Chapter 8—The Future is Waiting ................................................. 91**
  What to do after the job interview. ............................................... 91
  You Got the Job! Now what? ....................................................... 93
  How to Transform a Rejection into Something Positive. ............. 95

**Conclusion ...................................................................................... 101**

# Introduction

For most of us, we had to learn to crawl before we could learn to walk. The same goes with finding the job of your dreams. Before you can get the job you've always wanted, you'll have to get an interview for the job. And then you'll have to ace that interview, passing it with flying colors and positioning yourself above other candidates for the same job. Many great candidates have lost job opportunities because they either were not able to get interviews or they came up empty in the interviews they had. Maybe they didn't have a resume that stood out above other candidates. Maybe their cover letter was lacking. Maybe they didn't dress appropriately for the interview. Maybe they didn't prepare properly. Maybe they got stumped by a question in the interview or maybe they said something wrong. Maybe, maybe, maybe... In getting and then acing interviews, it's extremely important that you have a plan and a process which gives you the best chance possible to get the job you're looking for.

In this book, I'm going to give you the tools and techniques you'll need to score interviews for the jobs you're interested in. I'm also going to tell you the things you'll need to do in the interview itself, including how to prepare for questions, how to dress, how to navigate difficult questions, what questions to ask prospective employers, how to broach and negotiate salary, and what to do in following up after the interview. All in all, I'll tell you how to position yourself above other candidates who are applying for the same job.

My name is David Allen. I am a how-to-get-a-job expert. I have years of experience as a human resources director for multiple companies in different industries. I've also worked as a recruiter, recruiting people to fill various corporate job openings. And finally, I also work as a career counselor, helping people find optimum career paths or jobs that will enable them to live happy, healthy, and successful lives. Over the years, I've noted that so many people are unable to get the jobs they want, simply because they don't know how to get interviews, how to prepare for interviews, or how to perform in the actual interview itself. Many of my clients who have had success based on the knowledge I've provided, have encouraged me to detail my knowledge in the form of a book. With this book, I've now done that, in the hopes that I'll be able to help a lot more people in their efforts to get the jobs they want.

If you can implement some of the tips and techniques I'm providing in this book, you'll enhance your chances of getting interviews for the jobs you're interested in and, subsequently, landing the jobs you really want. As a career counselor, I've worked with clients who had been trying for years to get the interviews or the jobs they were interested in. These clients came to me because they were not successful in their efforts and they wanted to know how they could improve their chances of securing the jobs they were looking for. In following some of the simple recommendations and steps I provided, these clients immediately found that they were having more success in getting interviews and in the results of those interviews. Many of these clients were unaware of what they were doing wrong, the things that made them unsuccessful in their efforts. With some simple tweaking, I was able to help these clients get the jobs they wanted.

Whether these clients were looking to find a job in which they made more money, find a job which utilized their talents more adequately, or find a job which had a better work environment, I was able to point them in the right direction and work with them in developing a plan or a process which enabled them to be successful in their pursuit of the job they wanted. Through the years, I've received emails, phone calls, and handwritten notes thanking me for my help in this process. Some of my clients have even told me that the information and advice I provided was life-altering. I sincerely hope that I can make the same impact on your job search and possibly even your career. I'd be delighted to receive a note from you someday soon telling me that in this book I provided you with tips and techniques you used to land the job of your dreams.

If you'll read this short book and follow the tips and techniques I've provided, I'll assure you that you'll increase your chances to get job interviews and also increase the chances of getting the job itself. Before you can land the job you really want, you'll need to get the interview. Baby steps…you'll have to learn to crawl before you can learn to walk. And then once you get the interview, there are some surefire ways to ensure that you can be your best self in acing that interview. Getting a job is an activity that requires a plan and a process. Throughout this book, I will encourage you to develop a solid plan and then to focus more on the process of being your best self in trying to get the job you want instead of focusing on the results of your efforts. If you can develop a plan based on my recommendations and then work that plan, I'll assure you that you will enhance your chances of getting the job you really want.

I've read before that self-help or how-to books of this nature generally illicit two different types of calls to action: Some readers will tuck the knowledge that is offered into the remote regions of their memory banks, saying that they'll implement those ideas at a later date, whenever they get around to it. For the most part, these people are generally unsuccessful in their efforts, as "life happens"/time passes and they never get around to implementing the plan they said they would someday implement. The other type of reader is the type who will take the information gained and implement it immediately. I only hope that you are this type of reader, as these are the people who are much more likely to be successful in their efforts. If you'll implement immediately the tips in this book which are appropriate to you, you'll be much more likely to be successful in landing interviews and jobs. No, I can't guarantee that you'll get the job you're interested in, but I will guarantee that you'll have a much better chance to do so. Again, the key will be to focus on the process of getting interviews and jobs as compared to the results.

The tips and techniques in this book have been proven to be successful. If you will take the time to read this short book and then implement a plan based on the information the book provides, you'll increase your chances to get the interviews and the jobs you really want. Each chapter of this book has specific tips and techniques which can help you be successful in your job-hunting efforts. So, that being said, "Let's get after it"!

# Chapter 1—Score the Interview

Looking for a job can be a daunting task. It can be tedious, stressful, and disappointing. But, by breaking this down into individual tasks, you can make substantial progress in just a short amount of time. As mentioned before, you won't be able to get a job unless you get an interview first. With this in mind, this chapter outlines the best ways to ensure that you get interviews.

**How to Land More Job Interviews Immediately.**

Whenever you try to secure an interview with a prospective employer, it's extremely important for you to keep in mind that in, in almost all instances, you'll be one of multiple people applying for that job. With this in mind, you're going to have to make sure that you stand out from other applicants.

First of all, you should determine exactly what kind of position you want to apply for and also, if possible, what kind of company you would like to work for. As an example, if you have a marketing background and you are interested in a marketing job, I would suggest that you narrow your search within those parameters. A client of mine, who was looking to make a job change, had a background in restaurant marketing for two different franchised restaurant chains. He enjoyed different aspects of both these jobs, however he had grown stagnant with the restaurant company he was working for. So, in realizing that he enjoyed working in the restaurant and hospitality industry and also realizing that companies within the restaurant industry would value his experience, my client opted to look for a job within the restaurant industry. To narrow the field even further, he realized that his experience of working for a franchised company would be particularly attractive to another franchised restaurant company.

So, he targeted restaurant companies in his job search and narrowed the field even more by selecting some franchised restaurant companies in his search. He was fully aware of the things he could bring to the table for a restaurant company or a franchised company that other applicants might not be able to offer. So, instead of applying to be a marketing person in a tech company or an architectural company in which he had no experience (and not much interest), my client decided to target franchised restaurant groups. Also, it should be noted that he targeted a few companies which consisted mostly of company-owned restaurants and a few companies in other franchised industries, including a franchised health club chain and a franchised print shop chain. In other words, my client took a personal inventory of his experience and his likes and then used that information to determine the types of companies to which he wanted to submit applications.

Once he did that, he adjusted his resume to fit that particular industry or those particular companies. For instance, with the franchised health club chains, he mentioned early in his resume that he had considerable experience in working with franchisees from all different areas of the country. He was aware that the franchised health club chain, which had started in one area of the company, was now expanding to other areas of the country and he he realized that this experience of working with franchisees in different areas of the country would likely be particularly valuable to the company he was interested in working for. Although I'll give you additional tips on how to develop a resume that stands out later in this chapter, I'll tell you now that it will be very important for you to continue to tweak and adjust your resume based on the companies you are sending it to. No, you can't just develop one resume, make 100 copies of that resume, and then send it out for every job you're interested in. If you want to be successful in getting interviews, you'll need to continue to fine tune your resume for each job you're applying for.

Another way to ensure that you'll land more interviews will be to prepare and update your personal marketing materials before you even begin sending out resumes. Do you have business cards that you can hand out at networking events or any time you meet someone who could be a possible job source for you? Do you have a LinkedIn profile? (If not, you should have one.) If you have a LinkedIn profile, have you updated that profile? Are you present on social media platforms such as Facebook, Instagram, and Twitter? If so, do those sites convey you as a person who would be an asset to a company that is hiring? Is there any negative information on those sites that might impact your chances of landing a job? If so, can that information be deleted? Or, if it can't be deleted, is it something that can be addressed or justified if a prospective employer asks you about it in an interview? Do you have your own personal web page or a blog site? If not, are these things that might help you secure a new job? If you have a personal web site or blog site, make sure those sites reflect a positive image to a prospective employer.

In trying to determine which companies might be hiring, it's important to note that an extraordinary number of job openings are not advertised. I've seen research which shows that over 90% of all jobs are not advertised. Although this seems a bit high to me, the importance of the thought should not be lost…most job openings are not posted. With this in mind, I'll tell you that even though it is certainly important for you to search job boards when looking for jobs, you should never stop there. Companies often don't post jobs on job boards because they don't want to be swamped with resumes, many from candidates who are not qualified. Other companies prefer to solicit their own candidates through internal postings or by searching through resumes on LinkedIn or other job platforms and then inviting qualified candidates to interview. Other companies will hire recruiters, often referred to as headhunters, to bring candidates to them.

## Job Interview Preparation

And finally, in your efforts to find out about job openings and secure interviews, I strongly encourage you to network. Network, network, network. Even if you don't participate regularly with any organized networking groups or professional organizations, I encourage you to have a "networking mindset", which means that you are consistently telling people about the positions you are looking for. I always like to tell the following story, which comes from a client of mine. She was looking for an accounting job in a specific major retail store chain. Her research had told her that this company was a great company to work for, however she had no contacts there and no way to get her foot in the door for an interview. She made a habit of telling most of the people she knew that she was interested in getting an interview with this particular company she had targeted. Eventually, when she was at her hair salon, she mentioned this to her hair stylist. Sure enough, the stylist responded that her brother-in-law was one of the head accounting people in the company my client was interested in. The stylist asked for a business card to pass along to her brother-in-law and my client gladly complied. Less than a week later, my client got a call from the stylist's brother-in-law. This call resulted in an interview. After a series of interviews, my client is now happily employed at the company she targeted. The morals of the story: Network; spread the word; don't ignore any possible sources. Who would have thought that a contact with a hair stylist could lead to an accounting position in a major retail chain? But it did. If you've targeted specific companies you want to work for, don't hesitate to ask anyone you know if they know anyone inside that company.

Another obvious approach to get interviews with a targeted company is to simply find out who the hiring manager is for that company and then call them. If you're lucky, you'll be able to talk directly to the hiring manager. If not, you may have to go through the gatekeeper or the secretary to find out if there are any current openings. Even if there are no current openings, I encourage you to send a follow up note directly to the hiring manager and express your interest in working for the company. Ask them to contact you whenever there is an opening. And one other footnote: If there is a gatekeeper and you have a feeling that the gatekeeper is not forwarding your information to the hiring manager, you might try to call just before or soon after normal work hours before the gatekeeper arrives or before he or she leaves for the day. Many of my clients have found those before or after regular work hours to be the best times to reach hiring managers directly by phone.

And, whether you can't get past the gatekeeper or if the hiring manager tells you that there are no current openings, it's always important for you to follow up in some way, shape, or form, whether that's with a phone call or a personal "thanks for your time" note. Be persistent without becoming a nuisance. Your goal in any follow up should be to convey that you have sincere interest in interviewing with or working for that company and for you to create top-of-the-mind awareness as a possible candidate. This small gesture of following up can sometimes place you above other candidates when a job comes open.

## Tips for Building a Resume that Can Get You Hired.

Your resume is likely to be a key element in determining whether or not you are able to secure an interview. In developing your resume, you should remember that it will often be compared side-by-side with the resumes of other candidates. With this in mind, you'll want to make sure that your resume stands out compared to these other resumes. Here are some basic tips which you can use in building a resume that will get you hired:

Before you build your own resume, you should review other sample resumes, which are very easy to find on the internet. If you are looking for a job in specific industries, I suggest that you also search industry-specific resumes to see what other people are doing in the same industry. (LinkedIn is a great place to view resumes of people within specific industries.)

After you've reviewed various sample resumes, you should then find out what standard resume templates are available. You can find resume templates by simply searching "free resume templates" on the internet. Also, as many of us have Microsoft Word, that software program has free resume templates available. Take a look at some of these templates and determine a template that will work for you.

One of the keys in developing any resume is to make it easy to read. This means that you should use a simple type style, such as Helvetica, Times Roman, Arial, or Calibri. Nothing too fancy. Type size should generally be 10 or 12 point type, nothing smaller. You should limit your resume to one or two pages, nothing longer. If you want to use color highlights and bold or italic type in some areas, you should feel free to do so, as long as you don't overuse these functions. I've received resumes before that were loaded with bold, capital letters, sometimes color-highlighted and underlined. In viewing these resumes, I've often felt that the sender is screaming at me, trying way too hard to get my attention.

In drafting your resume, you should remember that in most instances you'll be tweaking or adjusting each resume you send, depending on the job you are applying for. In customizing your resume for a particular job application, I encourage you to read the posting or description for the job and then make note of the keywords within that posting. Those keywords should give you a good idea as to what qualities or experience the employer is looking for in the employee they hire. You should then try to work some of these keywords into both your resume and your cover letter, without being too obvious.

Also, if you are applying for a job at a larger company or a branch of a larger company, you should remember that many companies are now using a software bot to initially read your resume before it is passed along to a human. Some of these software bots are programmed to search for keywords. That's another reason why it's important to include the employer's keywords in your resume.

In listing information on your resume, also make a point to list important and relevant information first. In other words, if you're 40 years old, over 20 years removed from high school, you should not list your high school accomplishments near the top of your resume. List the experience, the accomplishments, the information which is most relevant to the job you are applying for. In listing your accomplishments, list numbers whenever possible. For example, if you had experience as a salesperson previously, instead of just saying that you were the salesperson for the North Central region, you might point out that you increased sales by 32% over the period of two years in the North Central region you were responsible for. Or, if you were on a salesforce of 13 people, and were the company's salesperson of the year, you need to make note of that. The more specific you can be, the more your talents and accomplishments will resonate with the prospective employer.

Also, you should use active/powerful language whenever possible to outline your achievements. Words like "achieved", "earned", "accomplished", and "completed" are examples of power words which can be used to outline the achievements and accomplishments in your resume.

And make sure that your resume includes your contact information. (Phone number, email address, etc.) It's going to be hard for you to get an interview if the prospective employer doesn't know how to get a hold of you.

And finally, please proofread your resume and cover letter multiple times to make sure there are no typographical errors or other errors. I strongly suggest that you have other people check your resume for errors. Errors, especially typos, are totally unacceptable on resumes and I know hiring managers who will discard any resumes that have obvious errors. The feeling is that if you can't pay attention to detail with a resume or cover letter, then you might not be able to pay attention to detail in the job the employer is hiring for. If you don't know anyone who is capable of proofreading your resume and cover letter and if you can't do it yourself, then I suggest that you hire a freelance proofreader to do that for you. Upwork is a freelance site in which you would be able to hire a proofreader, for maybe $5 to $10. Fiverr is another company that is a platform for freelancers, including proofreaders.

## Cover Letters: Why You Need One and How to Make Yours Irresistible.

Whereas resumes should contain "just the facts", cover letters offer you additional opportunities to make a "pitch" for the job. Cover letters allow you to expand on some of the facts you listed on your resume. They allow you the opportunity to express your sincere interest in the job opening and explain why you are a good fit for the job. Also, cover letters allow you to showcase some of your personality and to establish yourself as someone who stands out above the other candidates applying for the same job.

Some job applicants make the major mistake of ignoring the importance of the cover letter, thinking that the hiring manager won't take the time to read it. I can unequivocally tell you that cover letters do get read by prospective employers and you should never ignore their importance. You should compose a fresh cover letter for each job you apply for.

Here are some tips to consider in writing those cover letters:

## Job Interview Preparation

First of all, you need to identify the person you are sending the cover letter to and list their name in the salutation of the letter. Letters addressed "To Whom it May Concern" or "Hiring Manager" are not going to cut it. Get the name and the correct spelling of the person who is doing the hiring, even if you have to make a phone call to get this information. If, by chance, you're not able to get a name for whatever reason, you should at least get the title of the person who is doing the hiring. (i.e.—Director of Marketing, Human Resources Director, Accounting Manager, etc.)

As you write your cover letter, make sure you go beyond your resume. If you're just going to repeat all of the information that is on your resume, then you're diminishing the purpose of the cover letter. If there's anything on your resume that you'd like to expand upon, the cover letter offers you the opportunity to do so. Although you won't want to take up your entire cover letter in expanding upon something on your resume, the cover letter allows you a brief opportunity to do that.

It will help if you can come up with a great opening line for your letter. Whether you have a great opening line or not, early in your cover letter you should cover why you think you are a good fit for the job which is open. As an example, here is an opening line from someone who is applying for a management position in a Barnes & Noble bookstore. "I was excited to find that you have an opening for a management position at Barnes & Noble. I've been a fan and loyal customer of Barnes & Noble for many years now and, with my previous management experience, I feel that I can bring a lot to the table as a Barnes & Noble manager." In this opening line, you'll note that the applicant expresses their interest and enthusiasm for the job that is open. They also establish themselves as someone who is familiar with the company and loves the concept. (It's hard to quickly dismiss someone who is a loyal customer, right?) And then, the applicant highlights that they have management experience and notes that she thinks she can become a valuable part of the Barnes & Noble team. And, she does that with a casual tone, without being ridiculously formal. In two sentences, she's accomplished a lot.

When you are writing your cover letter, it's important that you are aware of the keywords which the prospective employer has used in their job post. In the Barnes & Noble job post, the company had stated that it was looking for someone with management experience. As a result, the applicant was quick to mention her management experience in her cover letter. Another example would be if a prospective employer says they are looking to hire a committed employee who can be a valuable part of the team. The keywords here are "committed" and "team". With this in mind, your cover letter might mention that you are a hard worker and that you work well with others as part of a team. In reiterating the keywords from the job posting, you'll be reinforcing that you are a good fit for their job.

In your letter, you should explain why you are a better fit than any other people who are applying for the same position. If you're short on the experience or credentials they're asking for, then you're going to have to emphasize less tangible assets, such as positive attitude, work ethic, employee loyalty, etc. In doing this, I recommend that you do not point out or mention your lack of experience or credentials. Let the prospective employer discover this themselves. Instead of saying, "Although I don't have much experience....", you should say, "I am willing to work hard to become an invaluable member of the team" or "As my previous supervisor would tell you, I have a positive 'can do' attitude, I am a loyal employee, and I work well with others." Again, don't apologize for lack of experience or credentials. Identify the keywords in the job posting which apply to you and then highlight the attributes you have that correspond with those keywords. (If you don't fit with any or many of the keywords in the job posting, you may not be a good fit for the job.)

Also, in creating your cover letter, please remember to emphasize "what you can do for the company" instead of "what the company can do for you." The hiring manager already knows what the company can do for you. Your approach should be to tell them what you can bring to the table if they hire you. Hiring managers don't want to hear that their jobs will feed your family, allow you to get the sports car you've always wanted, or place you on the career path you want to be on. Instead, you need to highlight what you can do for them and their company.

And, similar to the recommendations made for resumes, if you get a chance to use numbers to illustrate your past successes, you should do so. (i.e.—"As sales manager for the Northeast Region, I increased sales by 65% the first year and 32% the second year.") Again, remember that hiring managers like numbers to illustrate past successes. Tangible assets are usually preferred over intangible assets in resumes and cover letters.

Cover letters also offer you the opportunities for testimonials, although you should again remember that cover letter space is somewhat limited. If you get the chance to use a testimonial, you should do so. (i.e.—"My supervisor told me that I had performed like a superhero in organizing that event", "One of my customers told me that the assistance I provided had 'saved the day' ", "I consistently received top reviews for my ability to guide our customer service team", etc.)

I strongly recommend that you keep your cover letters to one page only. And even though you should have listed your contact info on your resume, you should list the same contact info on your cover letter in case the resume and cover letter end up getting separated.

And, finally, another reminder for you to make sure that you have proofread your cover letter before sending. Typographical or grammatical errors could well eliminate you from consideration. If at all possible, use an additional set of eyes to proof your cover letter and your resume. Enlist the services of someone who is good at proofreading.

## Chapter 2—Dress to Conquer

Okay, you've landed a face-to-face interview. What's next? Well, one of the things that is often overlooked is the decision on how to dress and what to wear for the interview. Although I've never been a "What to wear? What to wear?" person, as a career counselor I've seen applicants lose job opportunities based on the way they've dressed for an interview. With this in mind, here are some recommendations and suggestions on how you should dress for your interview.

**What to Wear if You're a Man.**

Unlike women's interview attire, men's interview attire is relatively straightforward. I always tell my male clients that, as an interviewee, their goal in regards to their attire should be not to stand out in an interview. If a man is standing out in an interview by the way he is dressed, it may well mean that the interviewer viewed his attire negatively. As a male, even though you certainly want to dress for success in any interview, your goal should simply be to fit in from an attire standpoint. Your ultimate goal should be to get the job based on what you say in the interview and what you have to offer, not on how you are dressed. If you think that a hiring manager is going to hire you based on the way you're dressed, unless you're applying for a job in the fashion industry, you're probably focusing on the wrong area. That being said, you can't disregard the importance of dressing for success and making a good impression based on the way you dress.

I'll never forget my first interview out of college. As a fresh-faced 21-year-old, I had the opportunity to interview for a public relations job with a major restaurant chain. At that time, many years ago, the company had all five selected candidates sit in the lobby at the same time as we waited to be interviewed. In sitting in the lobby with the other four applicants, it was immediately apparent that I was the kid fresh out of college and the other four candidates, also males, were older and experienced. I wore my only suit, my baby blue "interview suit", and a pair of spongy-soled dress shoes. The other candidates all wore more traditional attire, darker suits and more traditional shoes, including wingtips and penny loafers. I knew immediately that my interview attire would make me stand out from the other candidates, and not in a good way. But then again, I was less than a couple weeks out of college and I didn't know any better. I was fortunate enough to get invited back for a second interview for a job I really wanted. Again, as a kid right out of college, I was accustomed to wearing jeans and t-shirts every day and my "baby blue" interview suit was the only suit I owned. As I didn't want to wear the same suit to the second interview and I had no money to buy another suit, I borrowed my college roommate's suit for the second interview. Thankfully, we were about the same size; thankfully, I was offered the job despite my wardrobe deficiency. But I learned a lesson from that, and I made sure that I was dressed more appropriately for my subsequent interviews with other companies years later.

In determining what to wear for an interview, it will be helpful if you know what the dress code or dress mode is for the company you're interviewing with. Not all companies dress alike and you'll find that employees for a startup company are likely to dress different than employees who work for a corporate law firm. If you're not sure of what a particular company's dress code is, and you really want to make sure that you fit in when you are there for your interview, there's no harm in calling the receptionist at that company to find out how most people dress. I've even had clients who have gone to the company they were scheduled to interview with and, days before the interview, scoped out how employees are dressed with a reconnaissance mission in the parking lot. Although I think this is a bit drastic, it does point out that it's important for you not to look too out of place with what you wear for your interview.

## Job Interview Preparation

Hopefully, you'll know something about the company you sent your resume to and you'll have a feel for what kind of business they're in and how they might dress. If you're interviewing for the position of a golf pro or a landscaper, you can obviously dress very casual for your interview. As a matter of fact, you'd probably surely lose points if you showed up in a coat and tie. But for most other jobs, you may want to determine if the company you're interviewing with has business casual or business formal. The basic difference between these two modes of attire primarily deals with whether you should wear a tie or not, but also may deal with whether you should plan to wear a suitcoat or not.

Either way, I always tell my male clients that, if they're going to wear a coat, a khaki coat or camel-color coat is preferred over a darker coat. I tell clients not to dress like they would dress for going to a funeral. Pinstripe suits may be too formal, depending on the job you're applying for. Navy blazers may be more appropriate. Pants should obviously be coordinated with the coat. Navy, khaki, or even grey slacks are standard for most interviews. Whether you wear a tie or not may depend on whether you're going for the business casual or business formal look. Business casual is often without a tie, while business formal usually includes a tie.

If you're trying to straddle the line between business casual and business formal, a button-down shirt layered with a sweater is often acceptable attire, unless the sweater is the sweater you bought for an ugly sweater party. Again, whether you wear a tie will depend on whether you are going for the business casual or business formal look.

With your tie choice, you should select a tie that's not too bizarre, but it doesn't have to be boring either.

In choosing a button-down shirt, I recommend that you choose a solid color shirt or a pinstripe shirt, something that works with the other items you're going to wear and something that won't detract from the overall look. I recommend that you choose a long sleeve button-down over a short sleeve button-down, only because I know some people who are adverse to short sleeve button-downs for men.

Based on the rest of your interview attire, you should choose a nice pair of conservative shoes that works with the outfit. Nothing wrong with wearing brown shoes in conjunction with a business casual or business formal look. And make sure that your shoes are polished, certainly not scuffed. Also, a leather belt and conservative dark socks are normal interview attire for men, although with some of the unique and colorful sock designs today, patterned socks might work also.

And if you're a heavy jewelry wearer, go light on the jewelry unless you're applying for a job as a rap music producer. Joke. The same goes for cologne or after-shave. Go without or go very light.

And make sure your fingernails are clean and properly manicured.

## What to Wear if You're a Woman.

It shouldn't surprise anyone when I say that deciding what to wear for an interview is often more complicated for women than it is for men. Although I'm going to spend more time on women's attire than I did for men's attire, I want to caution women and tell them not to overthink the attire you decide to wear to an interview. Although the way you dress in an interview is certainly important, it is still secondary compared to preparing for the verbal parts of the interview itself.

How you dress for an interview will again depend on the type of company you're interviewing with. Dress codes for different companies can vary substantially. A startup company might allow jeans and tennis shoes, while a Fortune 500 Madison Avenue company might even discourage any attire that doesn't include a skirt and pantyhose. That's why it's important for you to find out what kind of dress code the company you're interviewing with has before you

## Job Interview Preparation

interview. Again, if you're not sure, you might simply call the company receptionist and ask about the dress code or standard attire. And, if you're still not sure, I would tell you that it's better to dress up instead of dressing down compared to the level of the employees there.

In most cases, I encourage women to dress conservatively. Nothing too flashy. Nothing too revealing in terms of top or skirt length. Normal conservative skirt length is just above or just below the knee. Select a conservative blouse or top that coordinates with your outfit.

Unlike men, accessories are more of a major factor for women. If you're a woman, you have to choose whether to wear jewelry or not. And, if you choose to wear jewelry, you'll have to choose what jewelry to wear. Also, you'll have to choose what bag to bring to an interview. In terms of jewelry, some people maintain that women should wear little or no jewelry to an interview. Either way, it's safe to say that you shouldn't overload the amount of jewelry you wear to an interview. I have a friend in the career counseling business who tells women that she would rather see them wear no jewelry at all instead of cheap jewelry. Also, in terms of the bag you choose to bring with you to an interview, the bag should be large enough to hold your resume and any corresponding paperwork, however it should not be one of those monstrous bags that we sometimes see. In my human resources days, I once had a woman that brought it bag so big into her interview that it took her at least five minutes to find her resume. In looking for her resume, she proceeded to empty her bag of its contents, piece by piece. By the time she finally located her resume, she could have had a garage sale with all the items she had placed on my desk, and, during that time, I had formed an opinion that she was disorganized. In other words, her chances of getting that job had ended even before the interview really got started.

Also, I encourage women to be cognizant of the amount of makeup and the perfume they wear. I would encourage women to go light on the makeup and to go without or go light on the perfume. It's important to remember that some people are allergic to perfumes and other people detest the heavy use of perfumes. With this in mind, the use of perfumes in an interview probably isn't a risk that's worth the reward.

Just as I advised men to make sure they had clean manicured nails, I encourage women to make sure their nails are presentable.

Clothes should be always be conservative, so as not to detract from the interview itself. The clothes themselves should be ironed and/or wrinkle-free. They should also be clean. No stains, holes, snags, or ragged edges. And beware of pet hair if you have a dog or cat.

Shoes should be polished and not scuffed. Whether you wear high heels or flats is up to you. Open-toe shoes are discouraged.

If you're going to a startup interview with a company that has a very casual dress code, jeans and tennis shoes may be OK, but the jeans should be clean and without holes and ragged seams. If you are interviewing with a company that has a very casual dress code, I strongly encourage you to make absolutely sure how casual it is before wearing jeans and tennis shoes to an interview. If you're wrong with that, your chance to get the job could be over before the interview starts. If you're not sure, then it's safer to dress up instead of taking the risk of dressing down.

## Six Things You Should Not Wear to an Interview.

Although many of these things are common-sensical, there are some definite no-no's in what you should not wear or take to an interview.

1) Bright, flashy clothes. Try not to look like a decorated, walking Christmas tree. Stick with more conservative, solid colors. If you're going to wear a bright color, such as a bright red top, make sure that the rest of your outfit offsets or balances

## Job Interview Preparation

the bright colors you're wearing. Again, the goal here is for you not to stand out for the clothes you are wearing. You simply want to look polished and professional.

2) Scuffed, dirty, or outdated shoes. This tip applies to both men and women. You'd be surprised at how many people pay close attention to shoes and I'm presuming that hiring managers are included.

3) Too much jewelry or too many accessories. If you're a man, take off the bling or tuck it inside your shirt. If you're a woman, no large dangling earrings. And if you wear funky eyeglasses, go back to your more conventional and conservative design, at least for purposes of the interview.

4) Outlandish ties, scarves, socks. This applies particularly to men, but also to women who accessorize with scarves. If you're a man, don't try to be the funny guy with an outlandish tie or socks. You're not there to enhance your future as a standup comic. If you are a bow tie wearer, you might consider a more conventional necktie. Although I think bow ties can be quite fashionable, you should know that some people still have an aversion to them.

5) Heavy makeup; heavy perfume or colon. Instead of wearing heavy makeup, or heavy perfume or cologne, I'd recommend that you either go light or go without. Some people are allergic to perfumes or colognes; other people are very sensitive to scents. You never know if one of the people you meet in an interview with be of the same kind. Also, go light on the makeup. Don't overdo it. Avoid bright red lipstick and dark

eyeshadow. A light coat of mascara, a touch of powder, and some tinted lip balm are probably OK, but don't overdo it.

6) Outdated or worn bags, portfolios, briefcases. Some people totally forget about the bags or briefcases they use to carry their resume or interview paperwork. Make sure that the vessel you're using is presentable and professional, and conveys the image you want to present to your prospective employer. If you're a woman with a bag, choose a smaller size bag and minimize the contents so you can easily find the paperwork you'll need during your interview. And always bring a pen.

Again, with any of these recommendations, you should know that they're not set in concrete. I always encourage people to be who they are and to dress accordingly. However, in choosing what to wear and how you want to look for an interview, always keep in mind the person or persons you might be meeting during the interview and consider what kind of impression you're making with the way you're dressed or accessorized.

## The Truth About Tattoos and Piercings.

So, you have some tattoos or some piercings. Well, you're certainly not alone. Almost 30% of Americans have tattoos and half of all millennials have tattoos. That being said, you're probably aware that some people still have some biases or negative feelings about tattoos and piercings and, with this in mind, you may have to decide how you're going to handle that going into an interview.

First of all, let me point out that with some jobs and some employers, it's not going to matter at all whether you have tattoos or piercings. However, some other companies may even have company policies in place regarding tattoos and piercings.

Before we discuss how you should handle tattoos and piercings going into an interview, I'd like to provide you with some additional information which may help you in your decision on how to handle. A popular survey site recently revealed the results of a survey they did regarding tattoos and piercing. They asked respondents if they felt that tattoos and piercings hurt an applicant's chances of getting a job. 76% of respondents felt that tattoos and piercings did indeed hurt an applicant's chances in getting a job. Along the same lines, over 37% of the people surveyed said that they felt that employees with tattoos and piercings reflected poorly on their employers. 42% thought that visible tattoos were inappropriate at work; 55% felt that piercings were inappropriate at work.

In looking at these survey results, there's no denying that there is still a lot of bias against tattoos and piercings, whether that's fair or not. It should be pointed out that peoples' age is a significant factor in how tattoos and piercings are perceived. As you might guess, older age groups have a more negative perception of tattoos and piercings; younger age groups are more accepting.

People who have negative perceptions of tattoos and piercings are prone to think that people who have these tattoos and piercings are, among other things, less intelligent (27% of respondents thought that people with tattoos and piercings were less intelligent than people without tattoos and piercings, less attractive (45%), and more rebellious (50%). Unfortunately, the perceptions of women with tattoos and piercings are even worse than the perceptions of men. Whereas some people perceive men with tattoos as being more masculine, more dominant, and more aggressive, women with tattoos are perceived to be less honest, less motivated, less generous, and less creative, among other things. Those negative perceptions are most certainly an unfair burden to bear for a qualified candidate. I list these seemingly unfair assumptions only so you can see what perceptions you're dealing with if you're someone that has tattoos or piercings.

## Job Interview Preparation

You may be a perfectly qualified candidate for a job position, but you may be stigmatized or categorized because you have tattoos or piercings.

In deciding whether you should hide your tattoos in an interview or to allow them to be seen, here are some possible factors:

1) Consider the industry and the position you are applying to. If you're going to be face to face with customers in that position, you may well have to cover your tattoos and ditch the piercings. Positions such as face-to-face customer service representatives, retail sales people, and bank tellers are all positions in which you're going to be working with the public on an ongoing basis and, as a result, your employer may not allow you to have your tattoos and piercings visible.

2) Research and consider the company culture. As mentioned before, some companies even have company policies against tattoos and piercings. If they do, you're going to have to make a decision on how important it is for you to exhibit your tattoos and piercings, both in the interview and on the job, if you get the job. If you're adamant about not hiding your tattoos or piercings and if the company you're interested in has a policy against tattoos or piercings, you should know that this may impact your interest in working for that company or their interest in hiring you. In other words, it may be a dealbreaker.

3) Hide them in the interview and then ask later. If you're not sure what the company stance is on tattoos and piercings going into the interview, it's probably best to hide them (if possible) for the interview. If you have tattoos on your

arms that can be simply covered with a long sleeve shirt, then cover them for the interview and if it appears that the interviewer has further interest in you as a candidate, you can always ask him or her if there is a company policy regarding tattoos or piercings. If you have tattoos that can't be covered, such as tattoos on your fingers or the side of your face, you'll certainly have to broach that in the interview as it's unlikely that you'll be able to cover your face or your hands in most of the jobs you apply for. Whenever I discuss tattoos in this chapter, please know that I'm presuming that the tattoos you have are not offensive. If you have tattoos that are going to be offensive to co-workers or customers, that's a whole different scenario and you may well find that those tattoos may prohibit you from getting a job and you may have to have them altered or removed before you can get a job.

4) Don't let your tattoos or piercings be a distraction in an interview. When you interview for a job, you're hopefully going to want your talents and abilities to be the main determinants as to whether you get the job or not. With this in mind, you won't want your tattoos or piercings to be a distraction in the interview. Getting a great job can be difficult enough without having your tattoos detract from the reasons you're the right person for the job.

In summary, please know that I always encourage people to be themselves when they interview. I can't tell you whether you should hide your tattoos or piercings or whether you should allow them to be visible. You'll have to make that decision yourself. However, I did want to arm you with some information and remind you that some people still have a bias against and a negative perception of tattoos and piercings. Depending on the company you're interviewing with and the position you're applying for, you'll have to determine whether exhibiting your tattoos and piercings will inhibit your chances to get a job that you're interested in. And you'll also have to determine whether the tattoos or piercings would prohibit you from doing the job itself. If the company has a policy against visible tattoos, are you going to be willing to cover your tattoos every day? If you're really interested in the job and you don't have a problem with hiding your tattoos and dissing your piercings, then I recommend that you hide them during the interview. Then if you and the prospective employer have further interest in the opening, you should find out what company policy is toward displaying these markings.

# Chapter 3—Prepare Like a Boss

In preparing for an interview, it's important that you prepare for that interview as much as possible. Preparation is a great way for you to overcome any anxiety you might have going into an interview. If you've prepared properly, you'll give yourself the best chance to land the job.

**How to Overcome Anxiety and Nervousness.**

First of all, let me tell you that it's normal to feel nervous or have some butterflies going into an interview. After all, that interview may well hold the key to your future and you shouldn't ignore the fact that it could provide the next step for you in your career or your livelihood. So, don't let the fact that you have some anxiety alarm you. It's natural.

With this section of the book, I'm going to give you some suggestions on how you can conquer your anxiety as you prepare for the interview and also in the interview itself. Most of my suggestions will revolve around preparation. If you prepare adequately for your interview, you'll give yourself the chance to ace the interview and land a job offer.

My first recommendations involve eating and sleeping. You should make sure you're well rested before you head into an interview. Get a good night of sleep. Also, lay off the caffeine, as it will only increase your anxiety. No caffeinated coffee, no caffeinated soft drinks. And, obviously don't drink alcohol before an interview. This includes not drinking too much the night before the interview. I also suggest that you eat something or have a light snack before going into an interview. I had a client who went into an interview with an empty stomach and, as a result, her stomach was growling loudly throughout the interview. She was so embarrassed that she couldn't focus on the interview. In a similar horror story, I had another client who ate a greasy meal before his interview and, as a result, he had to ask to use the restroom in the middle of the interview. Along the same lines, I've also had clients tell me that the heavy meals they ate before interviews made them sleepy during the interview. So, bottom line is that you need to pay attention to what you eat and drink prior to an interview.

Another way to reduce anxiety for your interview will be to make sure you arrive on time, presuming it's a face-to-face interview. If you arrive just before an interview, you may increase your anxiety. If you arrive late, you may be eliminated from the job opportunity before the interview even starts. And, if by chance, you find out that you're going to be late for the interview, you need to call the person you were supposed to meet with and tell them you will be late. You'd be surprised how many people show up late for interviews without informing the person they're meeting with. If you're not exactly sure how to get to the location where the interview is being held, make sure you find out how to get there. Use Mapquest or one of the other internet sites to get driving directions or use the GPS system on your phone to guide you and make sure that you allow time for possible traffic delays. If weather is an issue and is creating poor driving conditions, I suggest that you contact the interviewer before you even set out to drive there; then keep them posted on your progress if anything changes as you work your way toward their location. If the job is important enough to you, and the location isn't too far from you, I've had clients who've made trial runs in the days before the interview. But if you're doing a trial run, make sure you're accounting for the time of day and the different traffic levels during the time of day. I've had clients who did their trial runs during non-business hours and then when they travelled to their interview location during rush hour, the transit time was much longer and they found they hadn't allowed enough transit time.

Another way to reduce interview anxiety is to plan what you're going to wear ahead of time, at least a day ahead of time. I've had clients who have waiting until the morning of the interview to decide what they were going to wear for an interview, only to find that the suitcoat they planned to wear had a stain on it or was loaded with pet hair, the shirt or blouse they planned to wear had more wrinkles than a Shar-pei, or the shoes they planned to wear needed polishing. If you're running around trying to plan your wardrobe on the day of the interview, you'll most certainly be increasing your anxiety.

It's also important that you do your homework regarding the company you're interviewing with, especially if you're not familiar with them. The internet offers all of us the chance to research companies from our living rooms. If you haven't visited the web site of the company you'll be interviewing with, you need to do so. Also, please use Google or another search engine to see if there are any recent news articles that provide information on the company. I had a client who, when researching the company she was going to interview with, found out that the company was having some serious financial issues that she hadn't been aware of. Although this information didn't discourage her from proceeding with the interview, it certainly gave her some questions to ask during the interview. Another way to learn about the companies you are interviewing with is to solicit personal information. Do you know someone who works for that company or worked for them in the past? Do you know someone who works for a competitor of the company you're interviewing with? In soliciting personal information and even with searching for information on the internet, I always caution people to take their findings with "a grain of salt". The information you receive could be inaccurate or tainted, but nevertheless it should at least give you some food for thought and possibly some information or questions that will help you in your interview.

## Job Interview Preparation

Another way for you to reduce your anxiety is to prepare for the actual interview itself. First, make sure you have all the necessary materials to take with you to the interview: resume, copy of your cover letter, reference list, portfolio with samples of your work, certifications, licenses, business cards, and certainly a pen and notepad. Again, pay attention to detail with the materials you gather. No coffee or soda stains on your resume, no pens that you or your dog have chewed, etc. You get the picture.

Also, in preparing for an interview, you can reduce your anxiety by determining some of the questions you want to ask before the interview. If you think there's a chance you won't remember the questions you want to ask, write them down on a sheet of paper and take that with you to the interview.

Do you have a friend or relative who you can practice the interview with? If so, you might find that conducting a mock interview will be very helpful. Give your friend some questions to ask you based on the questions you think you'll be asked during the interview itself. People who do mock interviews prior to their actual interviews seem to benefit immensely from the practice of formulating and giving answers to possible questions. There's no doubt that this practice boosts confidence heading into the interview.

As you head into an interview, you may find it beneficial to "step outside yourself" and the thoughts of the interview itself. Some people find this extremely helpful, as they relish every part of the interview process. They greet and engage the receptionist, they say a brief hello to any people they pass along the way to the interview room, they ask the interviewer how his or her day is going, they focus on remembering the names of the people they meet, they focus on a firm handshake and eye-to-eye contact, etc. In other words, they break each part of the interview process into a separate event and, as a result, it's much easier for them to relax and cast off any anxiety they might be feeling.

## Job Interview Preparation

In the interview itself, I always encourage people to "slow down". When we get anxious, we tend to rush things and that can lead to undesirable results. I have a friend who is a youth basketball coach and during big moments of the games when his players may be experiencing anxiety, he always tells them to slow down. The same goes with interviews. If you have anxiety and the interviewer asks you a question, instead of blurting out the answer, slow down and take some time and think about how you want to answer the question. That should be helpful in reducing your anxiety.

Along the same lines, you should note that some interviewers will try to catch applicants off-guard by grilling them or interrogating them. For applicants with anxiety, this can really throw them off track. If this happens to you, you should understand why the interviewer may be doing this and you should also understand that he or she is probably using the same tack with other candidates. Interviewers will sometimes grill candidates in order to find out how the candidate will react to stress. If you know in advance that this is an approach used by some interviewers, you'll feel a lot less anxiety knowing what the motivation is and knowing that all candidates are probably being handled in the same manner.

And finally, another way to reduce your anxiety in an interview is to ask the interviewer some questions and let them answer. "Throw the ball in their court", in other words. Hopefully, you'll have some questions prepared in advance and you'll also be able to formulate other questions throughout the interview. You'll find that you'll have a much better chance to land the job if you can turn the interview from a monologue into a two-way conversation. Not only will you have less anxiety, you may well find that the interview feels much better about the interview if it is a conversation instead of an interrogation.

## Nine Things You Need to Research for Your Interview.

## Job Interview Preparation

Research is a huge part of the preparation for any interview. If you want to give yourself the best chance to land the job, you'll make sure that you've researched the job you're applying for and the corresponding company.

1) About the Company. You'd be surprised how many job applicants don't know much about the company they're interviewing with. When the interviewer asks what you know about the company and you respond, "Well, my brother-in-law told me it's a great place to work", that's not going to cut it. You'll actually have to know something more about the company you're hoping to work for. The internet and Google make it very easy for job applicants to research companies. Almost all companies have web sites and you can learn a lot about companies by browsing their web sites. You can generally glean recent news items, company history, and even company culture from a web site. Most web sites have an About Us page that will impart some information about the company. Some web sites will have links to their blogs or newsletters. You can learn a lot about most companies in perusing this information. By the same token, I would also use Google to uncover additional information about the company you'll be interviewing. You should remember that sometimes company websites provide a rosy picture of the company that is contrary to what you might find in searching articles or reviews on Google. Again, I should remind you to be prepared to take this information "with a grain of salt". For example, if you are interested in working for a certain restaurant and you find an article trashing that restaurant on Google, take that article with a grain of salt. It could be an instance in which someone is on a crusade and has an axe to grind against that restaurant. On the other hand, if you see repeated complaints against that restaurant or any other company, you can probably presume that they have a problem in that area.

## Job Interview Preparation

2) Corporate/Company Culture. If you read between the lines on the company web site or in the company blogs or newsletters, you should be able to get a feel for the corporate culture. If a newsletter describes the company's annual picnic and shows lots of families with kids, that might mean that it's a company that values its employees and their families. If a company is involved in a lot of outside charitable activities (raising money for the local children's hospital, building and repairing homes as part of Habitat for Humanity, etc.), then you can presume that the company culture includes charitable work in the community. If the newsletters refer to company softball teams, corporate outings, or corporate planning sessions or retreats, you have an additional glimpse into the culture of the company. You can also find out more about a company and its culture by viewing their social media accounts, including platforms such as Facebook, Twitter, Instagram, and LinkedIn.

3) Company History. It's good if you can gather some information about the history of the company. Maybe you'll find out that the company was started by a couple of college buddies in a dorm room or that a company's first fast food restaurant was started in Southern California. Whatever information you find may give you a better indication of where the company came from and how that relates to what it is now. And don't hesitate to "drop" some of the information you learn into your interview conversation whenever appropriate. It won't hurt your chances if the interviewer knows that you took some time to do your homework.

4) The Key Players. In researching a prospective employer, you should determine who the key players are. Whether that is the founder, the owner, the current CEO, or various department heads, it will behoove you to find out what you can about the company's key players. As an example, I have a client of mine who has been on a career track in restaurant marketing for a couple of decades now. When he researches the next company he would like to work for, one of the first things he does is to check to see what the backgrounds of the key players are. Do they all have restaurant backgrounds or do some of them have non-restaurant backgrounds? Are the key players mostly young or are they older? In reading the bios of one of his recent target companies, my client determined that two of the company bigwigs had the same college alma mater as he did. He also found that a number of them were heavy into golfing as a hobby. My client made a note of this, as he was also an avid golfer. And later on, when the opportunity presented itself, he mentioned his love for golf in an interview and it led to a conversational discussion with the hiring manager, who was also an avid golfer. Bottom line is that my client researched the key players of the company he was interested in working for and he used the information he gained to his advantage, finding common ground with the person who did the interviewing and some of the company's key executives. With the knowledge that his alma mater was the same as a couple of the executives and that one of his favorite pastimes was the same as some of the corporate executives, he was able to establish common ground and give them the indication that he would fit in with the company and its executives.

5) The Interviewer. Hopefully, you can get the name of the person who will be interviewing you and you can then do some quick research on them. If the interviewer is not listed on the

company web site, you can certainly check social media platforms and Google to see if you can find a presence. Again, you don't want to go overboard with this, however you might be able to find "common ground" between you and your interviewer with the information you are able to find.

6) Company Competitors. Most companies have competitors and it may be useful for you to find out who those competitors are and how those competitors might affect the company's position.

7) News, Recent Events. Part of this should probably be under the About the Company section, but it's also important enough to have its own section or mention. You can use the internet to find out all kinds of information about the company you'll be interviewing with. Recent news articles, blogs, or newsletters might tell you about new products they're introducing, new services they're offering, a new branch or location they're opening, their expansion into other countries, etc. As some of this news may relate to the job opening you're applying for, this information might be extremely helpful to you in determining why the company has the opening.

8) Reviews. Just as you search for news and information on the company you'll be interviewing with, you should also check reviews. This can often by simply done in Google by listing the name of the company and then listing the word "reviews" behind it. (i.e.—XYZ reviews). You might be surprised by what you find in reviews. For example, my neighbor's son was looking for a summer job between his first and second year of college. He wanted to work retail and he had a specific retail

chain in mind. Before he sent his application to the company he had wanted to target, he searched reviews for this company online. He was surprised to find out that the company he had been interested in was notorious for paying its employees less than many other retail concepts and a number of reviews from ex-employees revealed some reasons why it probably wasn't the great place to work that he thought it might be. So, in his particular situation, researching reviews turned out to be very helpful for this young man and he ended up working for another higher-paying retailer.

9) Inside Scoop. Along the same lines as the abovementioned reviews, you can get additional scoops on prospective employers by searching the internet. Glassdoor.com is a site that can provide inside information regarding many companies. The information provided includes salary figures, employee functions, company reviews, the hiring process, and other details you can use to your advantage in positioning yourself above other candidates for the same job.

Again, I'd like to emphasize the importance of doing your homework in researching prospective employers. In doing so, you're looking to find information which will place you above the other candidates looking to land the same job. In researching prospective employers, I always remind clients not to ignore seemingly unimportant information. As mentioned above in some of the previous examples, you might be able to use inconsequential information such as college alma maters or love of golf as a pastime to establish common ground with the person you're interviewing with or the company you want to work for. At the worst, you'll at least be able to show your prospective employer that you've taken the time to research their company. At the best, the information you find might be a keystone in helping you show that you're a good fit for the job you're applying for.

## Other Vital Ways to Prepare for Your Job Interview.

Here are some additional tips you can use to prepare for your job interview:

Make sure you practice your answers to common interview questions. Most interviews contain the "Tell Me About Yourself" question in some shape or form, so you should definitely have an answer prepared to that question. A commonly asked question which has been the downfall of many job applicants, is the "Describe Your Biggest Weakness" question. This is a difficult question which needs to be handled properly. You probably won't want to say that you don't have any weaknesses, as that may come off as cocky or arrogant. And you won't want to spend a lengthy time describing your weaknesses, as you'll certainly be better served by spending time on your strengths. When my clients ask me how they should handle this question, I tell them to list a specific weakness, but then to also explain how they are working to overcome the weakness. For example, I have a client who is somewhat shy, at least until people get to know him. He's in a public relations position, so his jobs have often entailed speaking in front of groups of people. He's never been comfortable with this, however he's worked to become proficient at it. So, when the interviewer asked him what his biggest weakness is, he replied, "I've never really been comfortable speaking in front of groups. However, I've worked hard at it. I've joined Toastmasters and I've offered myself as a guest speaker or guest presenter at various industry functions. I'm now to the point where I am much more comfortable speaking in front of groups, and I'm still working to get better, but I've improved considerably since I realized that I had some shortcomings as a public speaker. I'm to the point now where I no longer consider it to be a weakness."

## Job Interview Preparation

Another question you're likely to get in one form or another is, "Why are you interested in this position?" or "Why are you interested in working for our company?" Again, you should have a rehearsed and polished answer to this question. In answering the question, it's important to emphasize what you can do for the company and what you can bring to the table instead of what the company can do for you.

In preparing for an interview, I strongly suggest that you practice answering different questions that might be asked. And practice your answers out loud. It's one thing to have an answer inside your head, but it's another thing to hear how that answer sounds when you express it vocally. I have a client who tells me that he sometimes practices his answers in the shower, instead of singing. Other people will stand in front of mirrors as they practice answering questions. If you have a friend or relative, or even a loyal dog, who will volunteer to be a willing listener as you practice your answers, that will be even better. I've seen the results that mock interviews and practicing answers can produce and I strongly recommend that you include this in your interview preparation arsenal.

I also encourage people to prepare some questions to answer during the interview. And then, hopefully during the interview, you'll be able to come up with some additional questions to ask of your interviewer. It's OK to jot these questions down on a notepad and bring them with you to the interview. But make sure you stay engaged in the interview and listen to the information the interviewer is providing. You don't want to be asking questions for information the interviewer has already provided.

I also tell people to prepare an interview kit to take to the interview. This includes resumes, a copy of your cover letter, a copy of the job posting, samples of previous work you'd like to show, licenses and certifications, and a vetted reference listed. When I say vetted, I'm strongly suggested that you've already compiled a list of personal and professional references who you've contacted and who have agreed to vouch for you. You'd be surprised how many people list references without even informing them that they've been listed as a reference.

Your interview kit should include at least five or six resumes, as you can never be sure how many people you will meet during the interview process. And don't forget to include things such as paper napkins or tissues, breath mints or breath spray, a stain stick, a lint remover, and even an umbrella. In other words, be prepared.

If you're going to take a bag to your interview, make sure it's cleaned out and you're taking only the essentials you'll need for the interview. If you need someone to help you to carry your bag into the interview room because it's so heavy, you haven't cleaned it out enough. Joke.

And always bring a notebook and pen with you to the interview. That notebook can include any notes or questions you have prepared for the interview, but you can also use it to take notes and write down any questions you have throughout the interview process. Again, it's important that if you're going to take notes during an interview, don't overdo it. You won't want to spend all your time looking down at your notepad when you should be making eye contact and engaging with the interviewer. With the notes you bring into any interview, you should be familiar enough with those notes so you don't have to constantly refer to them. And you certainly don't want to read those notes verbatim. I also tell clients to pretend that they are a television newscaster, looking down at their notes occasionally, but spending almost all their time looking at and engaging with the interviewer. And yes, eye contact is extremely important. When you meet someone and when you interview with someone, you need to look them in the eye. When I was a hiring manager, I viewed this as an absolute must. Persons who didn't look me in the eye when I first met with them had already lost points with me.

Body language is important. Stand up straight, sit up straight, and act interested. No slouching or slumping.

Finally, if you're a person for whom conversation or speech doesn't flow smoothly, I suggest that you come up with a go-to phrase that you can use to fill space while you are forming your answers to any interview questions. Some people will simply repeat the question. i.e.—When asked why they're interested in working for the company they're interviewing with, they'll use that question to transition into their answer. "Why am I interested to work for the XYZ Company? Well, among other things, I love the industry and, with my experience and my enthusiasm, I think I could bring a lot to the table." Or, you could respond by saying, "That's a great question. I'd have to say that among the reasons I'd like to work for XYZ Company are the fact that..." You get the picture. If conversation or answering questions doesn't come easy for you, use some go-to phrases to fill the void while you gather your thoughts.

If you want to give yourself the best chance of acing your interview, you should make sure that you prepare for it. In most instances, you'll be competing for jobs against candidates who will certainly do their homework in preparing for the interview. You'll have to make sure that you can match or exceed their efforts if you're going to land the job for which you're interviewing.

# Chapter 4—Questions and Answers

Going into an interview, you can never be sure what kinds of questions you're going to be asked. To help you with this process, I'm going to use my experience as a career counselor and give you both some common questions and some more difficult and challenging questions you might be asked in your interviews. Although I won't be able to give you the exact questions you'll be asked, the questions I've outlined should give you a good idea of what you might be asked in an interview.

## 12 Common Interview Questions and How to Ace Them.

Along with the common questions you might be asked, I've listed some tips on how you might answer. Although you'll obviously want to provide your own answers, the tips I've provided should give you some ideas on how you might answer the questions.

1) *"Tell me about yourself."* This is a very commonly asked question, often used near the start of an interview. With this request, the interviewer is trying to get a quick overview of who you are and make sure you're a good fit for the job opening. If you prepare to answer any common interview question, this is the question that you should most definitely practice answering, again and again. It's an important question and since it will almost always appear near the start of any interview, you'll want to immediately try to establish yourself as a formidable candidate; preferably as a candidate who stands above the other candidates. In answering the question, you should provide an overview of your current position and then

## Job Interview Preparation

provide information as to how your current position is relative to the position you're applying for. Also, provide any other highlights from your career or background that relate to the job you're applying for. And, it's OK for you to include a few personal details that might help the interviewer to remember you and to separate you from the other candidates. i.e.—"And when I'm not working, I love to spend time with my family. This summer I'm coaching my nine-year-old daughter's softball team. I love it."

2) *"How would you describe yourself?"* When they ask this question, they're not looking for your height, your weight, and your eye color. Provide an answer that coincides with the qualities and abilities they said they're looking for in their job description. If one of the keywords in their job posting referred to someone who can lead a team of employees, you should then make sure that you mention that you are an excellent leader, someone who communicates well, enjoys leading a team, and is good at it. If their job post mentions that they are looking for someone who can take a project from start to finish without a lot of supervision, mention the fact that you can take a project and run with it in your answer. Offer only positive descriptions; try to correlate the description of yourself with the qualities they appear to be looking for in a candidate.

3) *"Why do you want to work here?"* This question offers a chance for you to show that you've done your homework and your research. With your answer, you can point out how the company products, services, history, or culture relates to your interests. For example, when my college student daughter applied for a seasonal position in a bookstore, she was asked this question and she responded in kind: "I love books, I love

bookstores, I love telling people about good books, and I love helping people. I've loved coming here as a customer with my parents from the time I was a little girl and I like the way this place makes customers feel like they're valued and welcome. The people who work in this store are always so helpful. I want to be one of those people." In my opinion, this was a terrific answer, as it told exactly why she wanted to work there. Admittedly, she was applying for a basic retail position, so she didn't get into a lot of specifics as to what she could bring to the table other than a "can-do" helpful attitude, but she's a college student and doesn't have a lot of work experience. If you're applying for a higher-level position, you can use more tangible and less emotional references on why you want to work there.

4) *"What interests you most about the job you're applying for?"* This question offers you the opportunity to tell how your skills, your experience, or your attitude match up with what they are looking for. Again, I'll remind you that you should think about what you can offer the company with this answer instead of what they can offer you.

5) *"Why are you looking to leave your current job?"* In answering this question, this is not the time to bash your current company or your current position. It's not time to pull out the crying towel or the axe to grind. Don't focus on the negative aspects of your current company or position. Instead, focus on the opportunities or the positives that new job would offer you.

6) *"What are you passionate about?"* Another opportunity to relate your interests and passions to what the prospective

employer is looking for. Again, go back to the original job posting and add any other information you've learned about the position you're interviewing for and formulate an answer that shows how your interests and passions fit with what they're looking for in an employee.

7) *"What are your greatest strengths?"* Here's a chance for you to toot your own horn. Again, your answer should relate to the qualities they're looking to find in a new employee. For example, if they are looking for someone who can create and implement new product introductions, you might respond, "I love developing new product campaigns and I'm good at it. I've done it at my current company and our product rollouts have always been very successful. I can take an introduction from the idea stage to the implementation stage and I can do that without much supervision. I consider myself to be an expert in developing product introductions and I think that's definitely something I can bring to the table in the position you're offering."

8) *"What are your greatest weaknesses?"* We outlined this question in detail earlier in this book, but I will again remind you that this is a bit of a trap question, as you won't want to spend a lot of time focusing on your deficiencies when you'll be better served focusing on your strengths. It probably won't be wise for you to answer that you don't have any weaknesses, as that will likely come across as cocky and arrogant. So, with the answer you give, you will ideally give an example of a legitimate weakness that you have, but then you'll tell the interviewer how you have worked to correct this weakness. Are you a person who can't say "no" and takes on too much? If so, you might note with your answer that you've learned to

## Job Interview Preparation

say "no", you've learned to delegate, or you've learned to ask for help from your team. Are you someone who prefers to do things yourself instead of delegating it to a fellow employee who might not be able to do it as well? If so, explain how you've worked to bridge this weakness. Maybe you've made a more concentrated effort to educate the employee at the start of the project or maybe you meet with the employee a couple times a week throughout the project to make sure that they're progressing as planned. Either way, whatever weakness you unveil to the interviewer, you should make sure you tell them how you've worked to rectify that deficiency.

9) *"What are your goals for the future?/Where do you want to be in five years?"* I'm not a big fan of these questions, but they're often asked nonetheless. In asking either of these questions, a hiring manager is most likely doing one of two things: They're probably trying to find out if you plan to stick around for a while or they want to find out how their company or their position fits into your long-term goals. So, in answering the question, you should again relate how their company and the job they are offering will fit into your plans. If you're interviewing for a restaurant marketing position and tell the interviewer that you want to own a tree trimming company in the next five years, that's probably not going to help you secure the job you're interviewing for. Along the same lines, your answer should never be, "I have no idea." It's doubtful that your prospective employer is going to be interested in hiring an employee who has no idea where he is going with his life.

10) *"Tell me about a difficult work situation you've had and how you handled it?"* With this question, the interviewer is

probably trying to determine how you handle adversity and/or to determine if you are able to solve problems. In answering a question like this, you should remember that stories are often more effective than facts and figures. If you have a story you can tell to show how you solved a difficult situation, it will be more memorable that any facts and figures you can relay. i.e.—An events planner has a wedding photographer cancel on her the day of the wedding... A major corporate client announces that he is thinking of taking his business elsewhere because he doesn't feel like he's been getting the proper amount of attention from the salesperson who works for you...You worked in a retail store during the holiday season, the line at the register was about 10 deep, and you had a customer who was loudly complaining about the wait. With any of these situations or your own difficult situation, you should detail how you worked to solve the problem. And, hopefully, it had a happy ending. And, ideally, this problem will relate in some way to the position you're applying for.

11) *"Why should we hire you?"* This is a question that normally appears near the end of the interview. If you get this question, you should consider it a final opportunity for you to reiterate what you can bring to the table and why you'll be a good fit for the job they're offering. Detail again the skills and experience which make you a great candidate to fill the open position. Also, don't be afraid to throw in a more emotional, less tangible statement, such as "I'm sure I'll be a valuable employee", "I assure you that I'll work hard to accomplish the goals you set for me", "I'm very interested in working here and I'm sure I can be a valued member of the team", etc.

12) *"Do you have any questions?"* This question also often appears at or near the end of the interview. It's not a throwaway question and you should never not have any additional questions. This question offers you the opportunity to cover any subjects which were not covered in the interview. Again, you should refer to any questions you had on your notepad before the interview or any questions that may have developed over the course of the interview. If all of your questions have been covered, take the opportunity to turn the remaining interview time into more of a conversation. You could ask the interviewer about their own experiences within the company, ask them what success would look like in the position they are hiring for, or ask them what are some of the challenges you might expect in the role they are hiring for. Either way, don't pass on an opportunity to show the interviewer that you're interested in the job they're offering by asking some pertinent questions. If you don't ask any questions, the interviewer may not think that you're interested in the position.

## Navigating Difficult Questions Like a Champion.

Don't be surprised if you are asked some difficult or challenging questions in your interview. After all, an interview is part of an elimination process and interviewers are looking for ways to separate the competition and determine who the best fit for the job will be.

When I was fresh out of college, I had an interview for a job I really wanted. I prepared diligently for that interview. I practiced answers to lots of different questions by enlisting my friends to conduct mock interviews. Over and over again, I rehearsed the answers to any questions I thought the interviewer might ask. By the time the interview rolled around, I thought that I was ready for just about any question imaginable. About three minutes into the interview, the interviewer asked me a question that left me totally off balance. Her question was, "If you were a tree, what kind of tree would you be and why?" Oops, I hadn't practiced for that one. Why in the world would an interviewer ask a question like that? I didn't have a lot of time to analyze why she asked me that, but I wanted to know what the method to her madness was in asking me that, before I gave my answer. I quickly determined, correctly I think, that she wanted to see if I was able to think outside the box and to see how my thought process was. After stuttering and stammering for just a short time, I replied, "I would be an oak tree. Oak trees are strong and steady and they're useful. Oak trees have a strong root system. When they're in full bloom, they provide shade for others to enjoy. And they provide nuts (acorns) that squirrels, chipmunks, wild turkeys, and other animals can enjoy." By the time I finished answering that question, I was confident that I handled it adequately.

Although there probably wasn't a right or wrong answer to that question, I was happy that I'd been able to provide some decent reasons why I would be an oak tree. I later joked that I was glad that I hadn't said I want to be a weeping willow tree or a sappy maple tree.

A client of mine reports that he was recently asked a similar question in an interview: "If you could be a superhero, what superhero would you be and why?" Again, I'm guessing that the interviewer was trying to determine the applicant's thought process with a question like this. My client, who told me that he really doesn't know of many superheroes, told me that he answered that he would be Batman, as Batman and Superman were the only two superheroes he could think of when he was asked the question. He said that he chose Batman because Batman is/was someone who is very protective. He works well with his associates, including his sidekick Robin and his butler Alfred. He is physically and mentally fit, and intelligent. He has a passion for justice and an interest in protecting people from injustice. My client then added that he was like Batman in that he works well with his co-workers, he tries to stay physically and mentally fit, and, as a loyal employee, he always wants to make things right if they're wrong.

Not a bad answer from my friend, I think. He showed that he could think through the answer to a challenging question and then draw it all back into how Batman's qualities and his own qualities would make him a viable fit for the job he was applying for.

In the previous section on common interview questions, I've already listed some common questions which I'd consider to be challenging questions. Questions like "Where do you want to be in five years?", "Can you tell me about a difficult situation you've previously had in a job and how you handled it?", and "What are your weaknesses?" are all commonly asked and challenging interview questions. How you answer those questions may well determine whether you move ahead in the interview process. With this in mind, I strongly suggest that you practice your answers to these questions.

For the fun of it, I've gathered a few other challenging questions for you to consider when you do your mock interviews. Although the chances that you'll be asked these specific questions are very minimal, you should use these questions to hone your thought process in formulating rational and reasonable answers to difficult questions. Although I won't list answers for these questions, as many of them are thought process questions that don't have specific right or wrong answers, I'm hoping that these questions will provide some food for thought as you prepare for your interview.

Here goes:

    1) *"If you were a car, what kind of car would you be and why?"*

    2) *"Why do you think you'd be successful at the job you're applying for?"*

## Job Interview Preparation

3) *"Can you explain the employment gap in your resume?"*

4) *"What can you offer us as an employee that other candidates can't?"*

5) *"If you could host a dinner people with four famous people, dead or alive, who would you invite and why?"*

6) *"How do you manage and prioritize your time?"*

7) *"Can you tell me about a time in the past where you were innovative or 'thought outside the box'?"*

8) *"How to you deal with conflict?"*

9) *"Can you describe an ethical dilemma that you've previously faced and how you handled it?"*

10) *"What has been the biggest failure in your life?"*

11) *"How did you make time for this interview? Where does your boss think you are now?"*

12) *" Have you ever stolen office supplies from a company you've worked for?"*

13) *"Can you tell me about a company policy you're disagreed with and whether and how you expressed you displeasure with that policy?"*

14) *"Can you tell me a reason why people might not like working with you?"*

15) *"What would you do if you won $10 million in this week's lottery?"*

And there's one more question I'd like to discuss briefly in this chapter. You may be asked this question or something similar: "What salary do you think you deserve?" This is obviously a key question for both the prospective employer and for the candidate, as if the amount offered by the employer is too low or the amount tendered by the applicant is too high, it can easily be a dealbreaker. As an interview candidate, you will have hopefully researched what salaries are in the job category you're interested in. If you haven't researched, you'll find plenty of available salary information on the internet, including sites like indeed.com, glassdoor.com, payscale.com, and LinkedIn.com. In reviewing the salary ranges for your profession, you should always keep in mind the cost of living in the city where you'll be working. Obviously, the cost of living in New York City or San Francisco will be much higher than it will be for a similar job in Dyersville, Iowa.

When you are asked this salary question, I would highly recommend that you don't give a specific salary. You should first ask the interviewer to confirm the salary range for the job they're offering. For example, if they tell you that the job they are offering is in the $40,000 to $50,000 annual salary range, you'll then at least have a starting point for your negotiations. In most instances, I'd recommend that you request a salary which is higher than the median, unless there's a logical reason why you might be given less than the median. (i.e.—You're less experienced than the other candidates, you're a recent college grad and the other candidates have had previous industry experience, etc.)

Ideally, you won't talk salary on the first interview unless the interviewer is ready to hire you on the spot. If you're applying for a retail position in a department store, you'll probably be discussing salary during the initial interview. If you're applying for an executive position, it's more likely for salary to be discussed in a later interview. In this instance, I would avoid talking salary and compensation package in the initial interview unless the interviewer broaches the subject first.

In reading this section of the book, if there's one thing you can take away from what you've read, I'm hoping that you now understand that the key to answering interview questions, common or challenging, is to prepare and practice. Although the questions you practice answering are likely not to be the same questions you get in the actual interview, it's important that you practice the thought processes you'll need to answer questions you're not familiar with. With preparation and practice, you'll be sure to increase your chance of acing the interview.

# Chapter 5—Make a Great First Impression

The first impression you make as you head into your interview can be crucial. I always tell clients that even though it's unlikely that they'll get a job based on their first impression, it's more likely possible that they could lose a job based on their first impression. People who make bad first impressions can lose chances at jobs even before they get a chance to explain what their background, their talents and skills, and why they are the right fit for the job.

With this in mind, I've provided some simple tips on things you can do to make sure you make a great first impression.

## Eight Things You Must Do to Make a Killer First Impression.

1) Dress the Part. In an earlier section, I explained the importance of dressing properly for your interview. Again, the main thing you should concentrate on is to make sure that you are properly dressed for the job you're applying for. If you're not exactly sure what to wear, you should remember that it's better to dress up for an interview than it is to dress down.

2) Show Up on Time. As mentioned before, you're certainly going to lose points if you show up late for an interview. We've discussed this previously. If you're going to be late, maybe because of unusually heavy traffic or unusually bad driving conditions, you should certainly call the person you're interviewing with as soon as you realize that you're going to be late. It's not a good idea to keep someone waiting; it's worse to keep someone waiting when they don't know you're going to be late. On the other hand, I've not mentioned before that you should try not to arrive too early for an interview. You should not arrive

any earlier than 30 minutes ahead of an interview. If you do arrive much earlier than expected, the interviewer may feel rushed or uncomfortable in trying to accommodate you.

3) Be Nice to Everyone. When you're interviewing for a job, it's important that you "put your game face on" as soon as you enter the premises. Be nice to everyone you meet by greeting them with a smile and/or a hello. This includes people you meet in the parking lot, people you meet in the elevator, people you pass in the hall, and certainly the receptionist. Two quick stories: One of my clients was primping on an elevator as she rode up to the third floor for her interview. She looked at herself in her compact mirror, made sure her teeth didn't contain any food particles, made sure her hair looked good. As she did this, she basically ignored the only person who rode up in the elevator with her. You guessed it, the person who rode up in the elevator with her was the person who she was interviewing with. When my client discovered this, she was frantic in trying to remember what she had done in front of the person she rode the elevator with and she was embarrassed to think that she hadn't at least greeted the other person riding in the elevator. Another of my clients carried on a conversation with the receptionist in the lobby at the company where he was interviewing. The receptionist wasn't very busy. It seems that her primary responsibility was to answer the phones and the phones weren't ringing, so the receptionist was open to a chat. After my client was hired, he found out that the interviewer's best friend was the receptionist and the interviewer routinely solicited the receptionist's first impression of the people who interviewed there. Thanks to his pleasant conversation with the receptionist, my client got some bonus points even before his official interview began. So, bottom line is, when you go to an interview, it's important for you to get into the mindset of being friendly to everyone you meet.

## Job Interview Preparation

You never know when the impressions you make will impact your chances of getting a job.

4) Put Your Phone Away. It's obvious that you'll want to turn your phone off during the interview itself. But I suggest that you put it away from the time you enter the lobby. I'll note below the importance of being engaged during an interview. You can't be engaged in an interview if you're spending time on your phone. Back in the days in which I was interviewing for jobs, I always found the time I spent in the lobby waiting for the interview to be educational. It was interesting to see how the receptionist greeted other visitors and co-workers. It was also interesting to see how the company's workers interacted with each other. In one of my interviews, in the 20 minutes I spent in the lobby, I noticed that the body language and the interactions of the people who worked at that company were unusually negative. As a result, even before I went into the interview, I was questioning whether I wanted to work there. Sure enough, the human resources person was out of the same negative mold and I left the building knowing that I would not accept the offer I received. I was glad that I had put my phone away and was cognizant of what the workplace environment was.

5) Be Engaged, Be Interested. In interviewing for any job, it's important that you show your interest or enthusiasm. I always tell clients to make sure they are engaged from the time they enter the door of the office or the door of the building in which they are interviewing. Pay attention to the things that are visible in the lobby and in the office of the person you're interviewing with. An average interview might last 45 minutes. Those 45 minutes could be a major factor in determining your future. With this in mind,

## Job Interview Preparation

any interview you have deserves your undivided attention and your undeterred enthusiasm.

6) **Be Confident.** It's important that you look confident going into an interview. Pay attention to your body language, your posture, and your demeanor. When you meet someone, make sure to introduce yourself, offer a firm handshake, and make eye contact. I've noted before that whenever I've been the interviewer, I've docked applicants who have a flimsy handshake or failed to look me in the eye when they're introduced to me.

7) **Make Sure You Know Who You're Talking To.** This seems so obvious, but I've had clients who've made the grave error of calling their interviewer by the wrong name throughout the interview. I had a client who addressed Janel as Jolene throughout the interview and I'm sure she lost some serious points for doing so. Make sure you have the interviewer's name going into the interview. It's desirable to use the name of the interviewer(s) throughout the interview, but you have to make sure you're using the right name.

8) **Find Common Ground, Make a Connection.** With any interview, it's important for you to make a connection or find common ground with the people you're interviewing with. Again, you'll probably be competing against other candidates in getting the job, and you'll want to separate yourself from those other candidates by possibly making a connection with the person who was interviewing you. From the time you enter the building, or the conference room or office where the interview is being conducted, you should observe your surroundings to see if you can find anything that will help you to make a connection with the interviewer. Are there company newsletters in the lobby for guests

to read, a company trophy case or history case? What personal belongings do you spot in the office of your interviewer? Family photos, softball or bowling trophies, college diploma, etc. Can you use any of these things to find common ground? Many years ago, I was trying to get the business of a man who would later become a big client for my company. Upon meeting him for the first time in his office, I noted that he had a baseball trophy on one of the shelves in his office and also he had a framed version of a Minnesota Twins baseball pennant and World Series tickets hanging on his wall. I surmised immediately that this man was a baseball fan and, as an avid baseball fan myself, I started our conversation off by asking him if he was a baseball fan. Sure enough, he was, and we found common ground immediately. To this day, I swear that one of the reasons I was able to secure his business was because we had a common love of baseball. Of course, none of this would have mattered if my company hadn't been a good fit for his business, but our mutual love of baseball allowed me to separate myself from other candidates immediately. I've had clients that have been able to do the same thing with mutual alma maters, comparing kids ("Are these your sons? I have three sons...."),etc. If you can find common ground or make a connection with your interviewer, you're likely to enhance your chances of landing the job.

## How to Instantly Stand Out Among Other Candidates.

As I've noted before, job interviews are a competition of sorts. There are multiple candidates for almost all job openings and if you're going to get the job you're probably going to have to stand out from your competition. If you don't, you're likely to be forgotten quickly.

When my clients ask me how they can stand out in an interview, I have a number of suggestions on how to do so:

## Job Interview Preparation

I've previously noted how important it is for you to do your homework heading into an interview. One of the surest ways to stand out in an interview is to know more about the company than anyone else. Most interviews offer plenty of opportunities to show that they've done their research and to show how much they know about the company. Obviously, the questions you ask during an interview can also show that you've researched the company thoroughly. If you don't show the interviewer that you know anything about the company you're interviewing with, they're likely to think that you're not very interested in the job.

Another way to stand out in an interview is to simply be yourself. I encourage clients to be themselves during an interview, if only because so many people are not good at pretending to be someone we are not. We're not play actors and if you're trying to be someone else during the interview, most interviewers will be able to detect that. Another reason I encourage clients to be themselves is because if they actually land the job, the employer is probably going to find out quickly who the employee really is anyway. So, as strange as it sounds, you can stand out in an interview by being yourself.

And here's an important way for you to stand out. Treat your interviews like conversations. Interviewing is a two-way street. You're not going to make a good impression if you treat the interview like a college exam or a police interrogation, with the interviewer asking all the questions and you dutifully providing all the answers. It's important that you try to turn the interview into a conversation. You can do this by asking related questions throughout the interview process. Again, as I've mentioned many times before, if you're going to turn the interview into a conversation instead of an interrogation, you're going to have to be totally engaged in what's being said throughout the interview. Listen intently and then ask questions or add comments as you see fit. A good way to do this is to end your answer with a related question. For example, if you're asked why you think you're a good fit for the job you're interviewing for, you might say, "From everything I've read or heard about this company, it is a company that cares deeply about its customers. I'm the same way. I derive a great deal of satisfaction in knowing that my customers value the products and services I sell. This company seems to do a better job of that than its competitors. Am I right in thinking that and can you share why you think that is?" Note that the interviewee has answered the question and then followed it up with a related question of their own, a question which is not a yes or no question, one that will hopefully help turn the interview into more of a conversation than an interrogation or exam.

Another way to stand out in an interview will be to provide an additional one-sheet summary, other than your resume and your cover letter, explaining why you're a good fit for the specific job you're applying for. I've had some clients who will present this summary during the interview and other clients who will send this summary after an interview. Some of my clients swear by this technique, regardless of whether it's presented during or after the interview. I've also had clients who have submitted 30-, 60-, or 90-day plans on what they would hope to accomplish in their first days of working for the company. These plans are almost always presented in the days immediately following the interview (obviously before the company has made a hiring decision). In doing something additional to just the standard resume and cover letter, you'll be able to reiterate your sincere interest in the job.

If the interviewer asks you for examples of how you've been successful in your previous jobs, I'll remind you again to use numbers whenever possible to document your success. i.e.—"I was responsible for increasing sales in the Northeast Region by 135% in the first two years I had that region." Or another example: "As a franchise development director, we went from 45 franchised print shops to 87 franchised print shops within a year. The company goal when I arrived there was to open 20 locations per year and my team and I were able to exceed that by 22 locations." Bottom line is that numbers work in illustrating success and achievement. With numbers, you can turn an intangible statement into a tangible one.

And, finally, another way for you to stand out after an interview is the send a handwritten thank you/enjoyed meeting you note. Yes, I said handwritten, not typed. Handwritten is so much more personal than a typed note. If the company is very close to you, you might even hand-deliver it. If not, you can send it via the US Post Office or a delivery service, but send it immediately, within 24 hours. And, obviously make sure your spelling, grammar, and punctuation are correct.

## Confident Body Language that Puts You Ahead of the Game.

So, you think you've done everything possible to make a great first impression. You're impeccably dressed, you polished your shoes, got a haircut, and manicured your nails. Yet, if you don't pay attention to the signals your body is sending, your body can work against you and impair the image you're trying to convey with your appearance. Body language is important. We all know people who can capture a room when they walk into it. In just a matter of seconds, people will form perceptions on a person based on their body language. So, all the time and money you spent for the new suit, the haircut, and even the new leather portfolio can all get blown to bits in just a moment.

One of the key elements of body language is proper posture. If you want to display an air of confidence, it's important that you "walk tall"…stand straight, chin up, eyes up. Certainly, no slumping or slouching. Nothing worse than slinking into a room.

I've already mentioned the importance of a firm handshake when being introduced to someone. Yes, there's an art to doing something

## Job Interview Preparation

as simple as a handshake. When you're introduced to your interviewer, put away your floppy fish handshake and replace it with your "big boy" handshake. Male or female, you should offer a firm, genuine handshake. That being said, don't shake hands so firmly that you're going to crush the other person's hand. Always stand, and never sit, when you are shaking hands. Don't pull the other person toward you with your handshake...it's not an arm wrestling match. And avoid sweaty hands. And beware that there are some people who do not want to shake hands. Most of us know some people who are germophobes who try to avoid physical contact whenever possible. If you run into an interviewer who is a germophobe, don't take it personally.

At the same time you're shaking hands with someone, you need to make eye contact with them. And continue to do that as much as possible throughout the interview. In making eye contact with someone, you'll exude a sense of confidence, genuineness, and sincerity. Remember that one of your goals for the interview will be to create a bond or a connection with your interviewer. Eye contact can help you do that. If you're looking down at the floor or over at the wall when you're shaking hands with your interviewer, you may well give them the idea that you're insecure.

Besides your posture and your eyes, pay attention to what you're doing with your arms and legs throughout the interview. Don't cross your legs, when you're standing or sitting. Don't place your hands on your hips when you're standing. Don't lean toward one side. Don't cross your arms over your chest at any time. Body language experts will tell you that's a defensive position that doesn't play well with the person you're meeting with.

And pay attention to what you're doing with your hands throughout the interview. If you're someone who does a lot of hand gesturing, don't do any pointing, as that can come across as threatening. Open palm/open hand gestures are considered OK. If you are a bit of a fidgeter, try not to tap your fingers or your toes during the interview.

And don't play with your hair, repeatedly click your pen, jiggle the coins in your pockets, etc. Some of those quirks or bad habits are likely to make a bad impression with the people you meet in your interview.

And finally, smile whenever it is appropriate. And don't be afraid to show those pearly whites, unless you have bad teeth. I can speak from personal experience in regards to facial expressions. People have told me before that I have a stern face. Since that look tends to make me look grumpy or unapproachable, whenever I meet someone in person now, I make sure to make an extra effort to offer a big smile that will make me more welcoming and more approachable.

So, in recapping this chapter, let me again emphasize the importance of making a good first impression in an interview. Although you probably won't be able to land the job with the good first impression you make, you could lose a chance at a job with a bad first impression. That's why you should not ignore the visual impression you are making with the interview. By paying attention to a few minor details, you'll be assured that you've not lost the job before the interview actually starts.

# Chapter 6—Pass with Flying Colors

As you interview for jobs, you'll have an advantage toward getting the job of your dreams if you have an understanding of what interviewers want to hear. Along the same lines, you'll benefit from knowing some things you should never say in an interview. And then, you'll also want to convey to the interviewer that you have the soft skills which will ensure your standing as a valuable employee and place you above the other candidates for the same job. (For those of you who aren't familiar with soft skills, I'll explain that in more detail later in this chapter.)

## 11 Things Your Prospective Employer Wants to Hear.

When you interview for a job, you'll likely be asked a lot of questions. Some job candidates make the mistake of not understanding why the interviewer is asking the questions they're asking. If you have a feel for why your interviewer is asking the questions they're asking, you'll find it much easier to determine the things they want to hear from you. Here are some things that interviewers love to hear from candidates, in no particular order.

1) *"I'm self-motivated. If you give me a project, I can take it from start to finish...and I can get it done in time. You won't have to micromanage me. I can work with minimal supervision."*

2) *"I take direction well. You won't have to tell me the same thing multiple times. If you tell me what to do once, you won't have to tell me again."*

3) *"I am a good communicator. I'll keep you and my co-workers updated on any projects I'm working on."*

4) *"I work and play well with others. I'm a team player, not a lone wolf."*

5) *"I can lead or I can follow. I do both well."*

6) *"I'm teachable. I'm quick to admit that I don't know everything and I'm willing and anxious to learn from others."*

7) *"I have the skills to do the job."* (Reiterate your skills here.)

8) *"I'm a good fit for this job and I'm a good fit for this company."* (Detail why you're a good fit here.)

9) *"I'm loyal. I'll be loyal to my supervisor and loyal to the company."*

10) *"My goals and objectives coincide with the mission and purpose of this company."*

11) *"I want to say again that I would love the opportunity to work here."* (Presuming that you're still excited about the job as the interview nears its conclusion, you should reiterate your interest and enthusiasm toward the job before you leave the interview. If you want the job, you should make sure they know that you want the job.)

## Eight Things You Won't Want to Say in a Job Interview.

Just as there are some things you should definitely try to mention in your interview, there are things that you should not say in an interview. I've listed some common mistakes people make in interviews below. Hopefully, these mistakes will give you an idea of what not to say during an interview.

1) *"So, what do you do here?"* Someone hasn't done their homework.

2) *"I know I don't have much experience, but..."* No need to point out your shortcomings and to display a lack of confidence at the same time. If the interviewer has your resume or application, they'll already know that you are short on experience.

3) *"I didn't get along with my boss"* or *"I didn't like the last company I worked for."* Trashing past employers is not going to be helpful.

4) *"How much vacation time do I get?"* This is better discussed in a subsequent interview when you are discussing salary or the compensation package.

5) *"I'd like to start my own business as soon as possible."* Why should someone hire you when you're looking to leave as soon as possible.

6) *"I'll do whatever you want me to do."* Sounds way too desperate.

7) *"How soon do you promote employees."* Again, this comes across as desperate and will probably make the interviewer think that you can't wait to get past the position they're hiring for.

8) *"No, I don't have any questions."* I've discussed this previously. If the interviewer asks if you have any questions, don't pass up the opportunity to ask relevant questions. Not only can you use the questions to gain any additional information you're looking for, you'll be able to convey your interest in the position to the interviewer.

## 10 Soft Skills and How to Demonstrate Them.

When we talk about demonstrating soft skills, I realize that some of you may not know what soft skills are. With this in mind, let me first tell you what soft skills are. Soft skills are personal attributes, personality traits, social cues, or communication abilities. Soft skills are generally a lot less tangible qualities than hard skills. Hard skills are specific job skills or certifications. Examples of hard skills are high school diplomas, college or trade school degrees, professional licenses or certifications, training program completions, on-the-job training, job experience, etc. Hard skills are specific and tangible job skills or proof of job skills. Soft skills are less tangible qualities that are normally not graded by degrees, certificates, or licenses.

When a company is evaluating your resume, they'll generally look first at the hard skills you've listed on your resume. They want to make sure that your hard skills comply with their requirements and also they'll probably want to compare your hard skills with those of the other candidates. For example, if they're looking for an accounting manager, they're generally going to be looking for someone who has an accounting degree and possibly someone who has passed the CPA Board Exam. Those are tangible, hard skills. If you don't have those hard skills, you're likely to be eliminated from the competition.

After these prospective employers have determined your hard skills, they'll then move to your soft skills. If you've "passed" the hard skill requirements, it's likely that whether or not you get the job will be determined by your soft skills. Below I've listed some of the most common soft skills that employers are looking for. As you know, most resumes and cover letters have limited space. Although I encourage you to incorporate your soft skills into your resumes and cover letters, I am aware that there's rarely enough room for you to list all of your soft skills. As a result, it's very important that you mention that you have these skills in your interview. In listing soft skills on your resume, I suggest that you label them as "Transferable Skills", as those are qualities that can usually be transferred to just about any job you're applying for.

For the most part, soft skills are acquired over a period of time instead of in classes or training sessions. Whereas someone can get a journalism major by taking college journalism classes, people generally don't get soft skills such as communication skills, creative skills, or problem-solving skills by taking classes. These soft skills are normally acquired by "learning through experience", or the "school of hard knocks" as some would say.

Soft skills are often considered invaluable by employers, as they are transferable skills that can be used in just about any job. Customer service jobs or jobs in which employees come into direct contact with customers are particularly conducive to soft skills.

In determining which soft skills you want to promote, you should read the posting for that position and you note any soft skills which are mentioned in that posting. These are skills that you should be sure to work into your resume, your cover letter, and your interview, presuming you have the skills they are describing.

For example, if the job posting mentions that the company is looking for someone to become part of their team or the key words in the posting include words such as "team", "teamwork", or "works with others", you'll then know that the company is looking for someone who has this skill. Almost all job postings mention at least a couple of soft skills that the employer is looking for.

Here are some common soft skills which companies are looking for in the people they hire:

1) Motivated or self-motivated.
2) Hard worker or strong work ethic.
3) Adaptability.
4) Team player, able to work well with others.


5) Communicator.
6) Creative thinker, think outside the box, critical thinking.
7) Decision making.
8) Able to resolve conflicts or solve problems.
9) Time management, ability to prioritize.
10) Positivity, enthusiasm.


Again, prior to your interview, you should review the soft skills which are mentioned in the job posting and take an inventory of your own soft skills to see which skills correspond to those that the prospective employer is looking for. Then, you should develop a plan on how you can let the interviewer know you have these skills. For example, if the posting mentions that the employer is looking for a hard worker and you are indeed a hard worker, you'll need to figure out how to drop this into your interview. It won't matter whether you drop this information into the interview directly or indirectly, but you definitely need to let the interview know that you are a hard worker.

If you can provide specific examples to show that you are a hard worker, that's even better. For example, a client of mine was interviewing for a public relations job in which the primary responsibility included events planning. The posting for this job had mentioned that the company was looking to hire someone that was willing to work hard if necessary to complete a project. So, during her interview, my client mentioned that she was a hard worker and she was willing to work whatever hours were necessary to meet the goals of the department or to complete projects on time. She gave the specific example of how she had coordinated a milk carton boat race in one of her previous jobs. (Yes, boats made of milk cartons.) Her company had been the sole sponsor of this event and her supervisor and the management team had underestimated the amount of time it would take to put this even together. As a result, my client and her two team members had to work 12-hour days, 7 days a week in the two weeks prior to the event to make sure that it went off as planned. As a result of the work of her and her team members, the event went off flawlessly and she received plenty of thank you's from company executives who recognized her hard work and a special thank you from the supervisor who had underestimated the amount of time it would take to plan the event.

As you can see, my client not only mentioned that she was a hard worker, she also told a story that showed that she was a hard worker, willing to do whatever was necessary to make the event a success.

I'll give you another example. Another company looking for a customer service representative mentioned that they were looking for candidates who were problem solvers. One of my clients was applying for this job with a promotional products company, a company that provides custom-imprinted items such as t-shirts, pens, tote bags, etc. for corporate customers. My client had previous experience with a promotional products company and he told this story when asked to describe a problem situation in a previous job and how she handled it. A customer had ordered daily calendar refills every year for many years. One year, the customer was delayed in placing their order and by the time my client went to order these calendar refills for her customer, the factory was sold out of them and they were not going to be getting more of these refills, as they were made in Malaysia and the delivery time to receive additional refill pads was going to be well into March or April of the upcoming year. Instead of just dropping this problem back into her customer's lap, my client worked immediately to find another factory that had similar, but not identical, refills that would work. She had to do about three hours of research and make about a dozen phone calls to come up with a solution to the problem, but she did. She then contacted her customer to make them aware of the initial problem and, at the same time, explain that she had found a solution. She immediately offered to send the customer a photo of the alternate calendar refill pads and the customer found them to be acceptable. All of this for a customer who was placing a small order of about $150.

This story certainly showed my client's ability to attack a problem and solve it, despite the small size of the order. It shows that she was able to go "above and beyond" to solve a problem on behalf of her customer.

If you can find a way to effectively communicate your soft skills to your interviewer, you'll give yourself a much better chance to land the job.

Job Interview Preparation

# Chapter 7—Finishing Touches

With this chapter, I'm going to tell you how to put the finishing touches on what will hopefully be a successful interview. I'll give you some questions you can ask the interviewer, I'll tell you how to broach the salary and compensation package discussion, and I'll tell you what to do when and if a question catches you off-guard. And we'll also discuss if and when it's OK to lie or embellish during an interview.

## 11 Great Questions to Ask the Hiring Manager.

As we've discussed before, the more you can turn your interview into a conversation instead of an interrogation or an exam, the more successful you'll be. Remember, interviews are two-way streets. The interviewer should not be the only person gathering information. You should also be asking the questions you'll need to know about the job you're applying for.

Toward the end of almost every interview, the interviewer or hiring manager is likely to ask you if you have any questions. As we've discussed before, the worst possible way to answer this question is to say that you don't have any questions. If you do this, the interviewer is likely to think that you're either unprepared or you're disinterested.

You should view this question from the interviewer as an opportunity to gather any additional information you're looking for and also to emphasize again the qualities, skills, experience, and reason why you're a good fit for the job.

Again, I strongly suggest that you prepare some questions in advance, at least a half-dozen. And then, as the interview winds down and you get asked if you have any questions, you should select two or three questions to ask of the interviewer. As the interviewer is likely to answer some of the questions you had prior to the interview, make sure you don't ask questions requesting information for subjects that have already been covered. If you do that, the interviewer will know for sure that you weren't paying attention to what he or she said during the interview. On the other hand, as you and the interviewer talk during the interview, you're likely to come up with some additional questions that are more pertinent than the questions you had originally intended to ask.

Below are some of the types of questions you might ask of the interviewer during this part of the conversation. A few quick things before we get into these sample questions: When you ask questions of the interviewer, try not to ask them questions that have yes or no answers. Ask them questions that they can expound upon. And, on the other hand, don't ask questions which are going to stump them or which they're not going to know the answers to. For example, if you're interviewing with the human resources person for an advertising position, you shouldn't be asking them technical questions about advertising methods or advertising philosophies. Those questions will be better asked of the ad director who you are likely to meet in a subsequent interview. And finally, although I'll cover this in more detail later, the first question out of your mouth should not be "What's the salary?" In my previous experiences as an interviewer, I had an applicant ask me this question less than two minutes into the interview. I immediately ruled him out as a candidate and cut what was supposed to be a 45-minute interview to a 20-minute interview. I also had another candidate ask, soon after he sat down, "So, what do you all do here?". I immediately knew that he hadn't done any research, other than maybe how to drive to the interview, and I ruled him out immediately.

Here are some questions you might ask in your interviewer when you get the opportunity to do so:

## Job Interview Preparation

1) *"Can you tell me a bit about the company culture or what's it's like to work here?"* This is something you'll definitely want to find out before you accept the position.

2) *"What are the next steps in the interview process?". "When are you looking to have someone on board for this position?"* And if you're meeting with a human resources person or a hiring manager, you should definitely find out who you'll be reporting to and if you'll be able to meet that person during the interview process.

3) *"Will this job offer an eventual opportunity for advancement?" "Can you tell me if any of the people who previously held this position advanced in the company or in their career path?"*

4) *"Is this a new position or are you looking to fill a position that someone previously filled? And, if you don't mind me asking, what did the person who previously filled this position go on to do?"* Or, you can simply ask, *"Why is this job open or available?"*

5) *"Does this job require a lot of travel?" "Is there any chance that I'd be relocated in this position?"*

6) *"What are the company's plans for growth and development? "What are the department's plans?"*

7) *"What's the best part of working for this company?" "What's the most challenging part?"* Again, another question that

might help you gain some additional insight regarding the company culture.

8) *"Is there anything I can clarify for you regarding my qualifications?"* This question might help you identify if the interviewer has any concerns and, if so, you'll then be able to address those concerns.

9) In the unlikely scenario that the interviewer hasn't explained the responsibilities of the job, you should ask. Along the same lines, you might ask, *"Can you give me an idea of what a typical day in this position might look like?"*

10) *"What's an average work week look like? Do most employees put in a lot of extra hours?"*

11) And finally, *"What's next?"* or *"When might I expect to hear from you?"*, *"When would you like me to contact you?"* or *"Is it OK if I follow up in a couple of days?"* Don't leave the interview without finding out what the next step is. If you leave without getting this information, you'll have to spend a lot of time guessing whether you're still in the running for the job or not.

## An Essential Guide to Salary Negotiations.

Depending on the job you apply for, you may have the opportunity to negotiate salary. Of course, there are some jobs in which the salary level is already set. My neighbor's son recently interviewed for a job as a seasonal salesperson in a retail chain. It's obvious that a position in a structured corporate environment like this is going to have pre-

## Job Interview Preparation

determined salary structures and you're not going to be able to negotiate your salary as an entry level employee. These are jobs that are what I call single interview jobs, in which only one interview is required before an applicant will be extended an offer or eliminated from the competition.

On the other hand, most multiple interview situations allow for some salary negotiations. Now, while we can all claim that money should never be the main factor in which to take a job, you also have to remember that the amount you're paid may well have an effect on how you perceive the job. If you're not happy with the salary you're getting or you feel that your salary doesn't properly reflect the talents and abilities you bring to the company, you may find that your salary (or lack of it) makes you discouraged, resentful, or even angry. If you're disappointed in the salary you're making, you may even find that your disappointment leads to poor performance.

In my previous work life, I worked for a company that was notorious for underpaying its employees. It was a great place to work…except for the salaries they paid their employees. As a result of this reputation, employees who worked for this company were the frequent targets of headhunters or corporate recruiters who were looking to place people in different jobs. At that time, I was a rising young executive inside the company and I held a position that carried a lot of responsibity. I was a hard worker and very good at what I did; even my supervisors said so. In this position, I frequently received calls from headhunters offering me interviews for similar positions that paid much higher salaries. As a 26-year-old, I wasn't looking to leave a company I liked working for, but I was fully aware that a higher salary might help me get out of the position of living check-to-check. I was hoping to pay off my college loans and then purchase a modest house. Some of the interview opportunities the headhunters described included salaries that were more than double what I was making and, generally, those jobs carried a lot less responsibility than the job I had. So, it was deflating to know that I wasn't paid fairly. I resisted the weekly requests for interviews for quite a while, but eventually my salary level tainted my perception of the job I had. I eventually started to accept some of the interview invitations and eventually accepted a job that offered almost three times what I had been making.

The moral of the story is that regardless of how unimportant salary might seem, you'll still have bills to pay and you'll still want to make sure you're paid fairly. If you're not paid fairly, you'll probably find that your lack of salary will likely impact your attitude and possibly affect your performance.

Hopefully, you'll have an idea going into the interview what the "market rates" are for the job you're interested in. If you're not sure, you can use various internet sites to obtain salary information. Sites such as indeed.com, glassdoor.com, and LinkedIn all offer industry salary information that you can use as a guideline.

It's important to note that salary is generally discussed near the end of an interview situation. In a multiple interview situation, you might first have a phone interview and/or a video interview before you actually interview with someone face to face. In these instances, you'll find that salary is rarely discussed in the initial interviews. That being said, you should never wait until the very end of an interview to discuss salary or the compensation package. Salary should not be an afterthought and, if you wait too long to discuss salary, you'll lose some of the leverage you might have in negotiating it.

Normally the interviewer will be first to broach the topic, but if they are not doing that and it seems like it's time to discuss salary, you can segue into this discussion by asking something like, "Would now be a good time to talk salary?"

Ideally, you'll be able to get the interviewer to give you a salary range before you have to give up too much information regarding your salary requirements. Some interviewers are likely to ask you what your salary is in your current position. If you're asked this question, I encourage you to be careful not to impart too much information. If you blurt out your current salary, you'll almost certainly be restricting the salary you would be offered in the new job. For example, if you're making an annual salary of $40,000 and you tell the interviewer that, you're likely not to get a salary that exceeds your existing salary by more than 10%. Research shows that many employers are reluctant to increase salaries of new employees substantially if they know the new employee's current salary level and they feel that an increase of around 10% is enough to get someone to leave another job.

So, ideally, you will ask the prospective employer if they have a salary range in mind for the job. If they continue to press you for your current salary, you might respond by saying, "What I make in my current position really isn't relevant, as this would be a different job with a different company and different responsibilities. I'm just looking for a job that will pay me fairly based on my talents and abilities." And then you might add the question, "Can you tell me what kind of budget range you have for this position?"

It should be noted that I would never recommend that you lie about your current salary. Although some people do that, and do it successfully, you should know that if you get caught in a lie, you'll blow your chance to get the job immediately. Also remember that you might have filled out an application on which you were asked to list your current salary. In filling out this portion of an application, I tell my clients to list their desired salary on this line of the application. I.e.—(Desired salary range is $50,000/year.)

So, again, try not to volunteer your current salary information too quickly (unless you're already paid about market rate. In disclosing your salary, you're likely to lose some of your leverage in negotiating a higher salary.

## What to Do When You Get a Question that Throws You Off-Guard.

Regardless of how long or how hard you prepare for an interview, you're likely to get one or two questions that will throw you off-guard. Don't let these questions fluster you or "throw you for a loop". I have some simple tips which will allow you more time to gather your thoughts.

You can buy more time to develop your answer by simply acknowledging the question. Here are some sample acknowledgments:

*-- "Oh, that's a good question."*

*-- "Oh, I've never been asked that before."*

*-- "Let me think about that for a moment."*

*--If you think you can come up with a good answer to the question, you might say, "I'm glad you asked that."*

Another way to buy more time is to simply rephrase or repeat the question. "If I were a tree, what kind of tree would I be and why?" or "So, what kind of tree would I be?"

And, if you don't totally understand the question, you can ask the interviewer to clarify the question. "I want to make sure I understand the question. Can I ask you to expand on that or to clarify?"

And, finally, if the question asked of you is a multi-layered question, feel free to jot down some notes as to how you might answer. But if you're taking notes, make sure that you take them quickly. You won't want to hold up the interview while you take notes.

## Is It OK to Lie?; When Is It OK to Lie in an Interview?

It's no secret that some people lie in interviews. Maybe it's the pressure of getting that job that you really want. Maybe it's the idea, sometimes true, that lying, embellishing, or omitting certain information from an interview will help you get the job.

Although I strongly discourage you from lying to your prospective employer, there might be things you can embellish or omit certain information in an interview. I'll give you some examples, in no particular order:

1) Salary. This is the number one thing that people lie about in their interviews. I recommend against this, as it could come back to bite you later, especially if the human resources department from your new company checks your references and the question of your salary comes up. Instead of making up a salary that is higher than you receive in your current position, you might put a price tag on your current compensation package, including salary, vacation time, benefits, etc. i.e.—"I have a compensation and benefits package that I would value near $150,000."

2) Your talents and abilities. Some people will lie about what they can do. For example, when asked if they are familiar with a particular software program, they might indicate that they are familiar with it when they don't know how to use this. If this is something you can take a crash course on and learn between the interview and your start date, you

could probably get away with it. But if you're not familiar with the program and can't learn it quickly, you're going to be in trouble when you are actually on the job and your employer expects you to know how to use the program. You'll be better off being honest and telling the interviewer that you are not familiar with the program, but that you are a fast and willing learner and willing to learn that skill quickly. I knew a graphic designer who lied about the graphic programs he was familiar with. He was hired for the job. But two days into the job, his employer figured out that the new employee wasn't familiar with the graphics programs he said he was, and that graphic artist was terminated less than a week into his new job.

3) How you feel about your current boss or co-workers. This is an area in which you can do some harm to yourself. If you had major conflicts with current or past bosses or co-workers, you will not benefit from trashing them in your interview. No, you certainly don't have to sing their praises, however you won't accomplish anything by trashing them either.

4) Your greatest weaknesses. If a prospective employer inquires about what your greatest weaknesses are, it's probably OK for you to highlight a weakness other than your greatest weakness. Instead of admitting a weakness that can't be corrected easily, you should select a weakness that you can or maybe have already improved upon. i.e.— "I previously took on more projects than I could handle, without delegating. I realized that shortcoming and have since worked to utilize my team much better. Although,

I'm still working on this, I now feel like I've improved to the level where it's no longer a problem."

5) Who you know. It's OK to drop names during an interview, but make sure that you at least know the person you say you know, as this is yet another thing that can come back to bite you if you lie.

6) Your interests. If you're asked what your main interests are outside of work, it's probably OK to select lesser interests that make you look better to a prospective employer. Although, beware. I knew a young man who professed that he loved to golf, when he saw golf trophies in the interviewer's office. He didn't golf at all and soon after he was hired, the interviewer kept asking him if he wanted to join in a round of golf. The young man continued to decline, but he told me that the interviewer who was now his co-worker eventually figured out that the young man was not a golfer and, although the young man wasn't fired, he was embarrassed by the situation.

7) Fired or quit. If you were fired or laid off from your past position, be honest about it, but don't dwell on it. Focus on the positive and tell your employer that you're ready for new challenges and opportunities.

8) Places you've worked. If you've had places you've worked at for short periods of time or places where you had a bad experience, it's OK for you to leave that off your resume or out of the interview conversation, as long as you can explain any employment gaps in your resume.

Again, no one can tell you whether you should lie, embellish, or omit information during your interview. You'll have to determine this based on your ethics and the principles you live by. However, if you do lie or embellish, I strongly suggest that you examine the possible consequences of doing so.

# Chapter 8—The Future is Waiting

Your interview is over. You either got the job or you didn't, or you'll have to wait for the prospective employer to make a decision. Either way, there are some things you should do to follow up on your interview.

## What to do after the job interview.

Before you hang up the phone, sign off from a video call, or leave the interview, it's extremely important for you to ask the interviewer when to follow up (presuming they didn't announce a decision before the interview ended). If you interviewed with multiple people, find out who you should follow up with and how the interviewer would prefer that you follow up. (Do they want you to call, do they want you to email them?, etc.)

After you've cleared your head, I suggest that you sit down and write or type some notes from the interview. As days pass after an interview, you're likely to forget some of the things that were discussed during the interview and you'll probably find it beneficial to have some notes which you can refer back to, if necessary.

After you've done that, you should plan to send a thank you note to each person you interviewed with. If you had a phone interview or a video interview, an emailed thank you note is appropriate. If you've had a face-to-face interview, I would recommend that you send an email thank you that same day and then a handwritten snail mail thank you that day or the following day. If you are emailing thank you notes to multiple people, write a personal and different note to each person you interviewed with. Preferably not the same note copied. An emailed note will afford you the opportunity to reiterate your interest in the job and emphasize again why you are the right fit for the job. The snail mail note should be much shorter, probably on a thank you card of some kind. With both note forms, I recommend that you always thank the interviewers for their time, tell them that you enjoyed learning more about the position and the company, and again express your interest and enthusiasm for the job they are offering.

In sending thank you notes, you should note that you're probably not going to get a job based on a thank you note, but if you don't send a note, you could lose the job. Thank you notes offer applicants the chance to stay "top of mind" with interviewers and if you don't send a thank you not or follow up as agreed upon, the interviewer may well think that you're not interested in the job.

If you are working with a corporate recruiter or a headhunter in your job search, ask your recruiter to follow up with a phone call to the hiring manager. They should be able to find out how you did in the interview. Even if you're working with a recruiter, the thank you notes need to come from you and not the recruiter. The interviewer needs to understand that you're interested in the job, not just that the recruiter is interested in placing you. And, if you're using a recruiter, I suggest that you personally follow up with the interviewer instead of leaving the task solely to the recruiter.

Hopefully, you've made note of when the interviewer asked you to follow up with them. A couple of notes regarding these follow-ups. Follow up when the interview told you to follow up. Not sooner, not later. You may have to walk a fine line between seeming interested in the job and seeming desperate or becoming a nuisance. When following up, ask them for an update on where they are in the hiring process and with each call or email ask them when you should contact them again to get an updated status. And, if it feels appropriate, you might ask them how you are stacking up against the other candidates they've interviewed. If you can get an answer on this, you'll have a better inkling as to what your chances are to get the job.

And while you are waiting to hear on one job, don't let that stop you from searching for other jobs. Depending on what positions you're interviewing for, getting a job can sometimes be a numbers game and there's no harm in interviewing for multiple jobs at the same time. If you get an offer on one job while you're waiting to hear on another job that you would prefer more, you'll then have a decision to make, but that will be a nice problem to have.

## You Got the Job! Now what?

Bingo! You got the job! That great news should sets in motion the things you'll need to do to transition from you old job to your new job.

Upon receiving a job offer, you should confirm the offer with a letter of acceptance. In the letter, you should confirm the agreed-upon start date, salary, and entire compensation package (if the employer hasn't already confirmed these things in writing with their offer). Make a copy of your letter of acceptance for future reference if questions should arise later.

Then you will need to tell your current boss that you have accepted a position with another company. You can do this verbally or with a formal letter of resignation. When you are submitting a letter of resignation, you should also copy the human resources person in your company. If you're initially informing your boss of your new job in writing, you should then offer to meet with him or her at their convenience to establish a transition plan. You should know that there are some companies who will not allow you to continue to work there after you've submitted a letter of resignation. Don't take this personally, as some companies have that policy and it shouldn't be taken personally. A client of mine hosts a radio talk show. When he got a job at another station three years ago, station management told him that he would not be allowed on air anymore. He'd worked there for seven years and he took that as a personal affront, disappointed that he would not be allowed to say goodbye to all the people who had loyally listened to his radio show over the years. I told him not to take that personally, as it was simply company policy. (The station was owned by a media conglomerate that had previously been burned by allowing a departing employee to continue on the air waves after that employee had tendered his resignation. The employee proceeded to "trash" the station with lots of negative comments during his final radio show. Thus, there was a reason for the company policy.)

In any letter of resignation or any of your actions following your resignation, I strongly suggest that you take the high road and remain gracious throughout the process, even if you had things about working there that you didn't like. It's never good to burn bridges in leaving a job. That might make you feel better, but it will also show a lack of respect for the people who continue to work there and you never know if you'll need something from one of those people in the future. Any letter of resignation should note that you were happy for the opportunity to work there and that you wish them success in the future (even if you might not).

In meeting with your soon-to-be former boss or supervisor, it will be good if you can agree on a transition plan. Will your supervisor want you to train someone else for the position you're leaving? Will he want you to provide detailed instructions for your replacement? I've had many clients who have been quick to offer their new contact information to their former supervisor, telling them that they are welcome to call any time they have questions regarding the position they left. If you don't think that your previous employer will become a nuisance with lots of phone calls, this is probably OK. However, if you're going to do this, you should be aware that it is possible that your new employer may frown upon this practice and you might want to instruct your old supervisor to contact you after hours. An exception to making such an offer to your old company would be if you've gone to work for a competitor. If this is the case, it's probably not even ethical for you to help your previous company and your new employer is almost sure to frown upon the idea of you helping your old employer.

Throughout the transition process at the company you're leaving, I suggest that you continue to maintain occasional contact with your new company, just to make sure everything continues to be "go". And, if you have any new questions that come up while you are waiting to start your new job, these occasional contacts will be good times to ask those questions of your future employer.

And finally, as you prepare to leave your old job for the new job, I'll remind you once again to "take the high road". Don't diss the company you're leaving, don't flaunt your new job to the co-workers you're leaving behind, and don't coast in your last days there. Continue to work hard, continue to display a positive and grateful attitude, and take the time to thank any people there who were helpful to you. Make the most of your remaining time there and create a smooth and pleasant transition from your old job to the exciting next chapter of your career.

## How to Transform a Rejection into Something Positive.

So, you just got the dreaded "we've decided to go in a different direction" news. You're not going to get that job you had wanted so badly. What do you do now?

Well, first you should realize that life isn't all puppy dogs and balloons. We all get rejected at one time or another. One of the most difficult things about being a job applicant is that ultimately whether you get hired is beyond your control. I know people who swear that they did the best they could possibly do and it still wasn't enough to get the job. Some of those people even think they had the perfect interview; there was nothing they could have done better. Maybe they didn't have as much experience as other candidates, maybe they didn't have the skills that other candidates had. Either way, they didn't get the job.

I always encourage people who have been rejected in a job interview to maintain a positive attitude, to continue to focus on the process and not the results, and to look back and analyze the interview to see if there was anything they could have done better or could be doing better.

Here are some suggestions on things you can do after you've been rejected in an interview:

1) Ask for feedback. After you've been told that the company you interviewed with has decided to go in a different direction, ask for their feedback as to why you didn't get the job. Ask this in a positive manner, not a defensive manner, and you might be surprised at how many hiring managers are forthcoming about why you didn't get the job. And, if you are working through a recruiter or headhunter to get a job, the same applies. Ask them to follow up with the employer to see where and why you came up short. You can use this information to evaluate the way you're interviewing. If you get rejected from multiple jobs for the same or similar reasons, you'll probably need to look at how you're interviewing or the positions you're interviewing for.

2) Analyze, identify, and adapt. It's important that you continue to analyze why you're not getting the jobs you're applying for. As mentioned above, if you can get feedback from the people you interviewed with, that will certainly help. But whether you get feedback from interviewers or not, you should constantly be analyzing your process and your performance in trying to get the jobs you want. Sure, it's possible that you might not be doing anything wrong at all, however you'll be selling yourself short if you don't at least step back and look for areas you could improve upon in your interviewing efforts.

3) Focus on things you can change. In some instances, you won't be able to make any changes based on the reason you didn't get the job. For example, I have a client from Illinois who recently applied for a sale position with a national firm. The sales position was responsible for two states, Louisiana and Texas. When my client found out that the company he interviewed with had decided to go in a different direction, he asked the hiring manager if there was a reason they hadn't chosen him. The hiring manager noted that the candidate who was hired, had previous sales experience in those states and that's why they decided to go with him instead of my client. Well, this was something that was certainly beyond my client's control. He couldn't control where his territories were, and he had no knowledge of that going into the interview. Also, it was mere coincidence that the person who got the job had worked previously in those Louisiana and Texas. So, my client probably didn't do anything wrong in his interview process. Someone else was just lucky enough to have worked in those states before.

## Job Interview Preparation

I'll giving you another story which illustrates how an applicant focused on the shortcomings he could change. A relative of mine is a baseball coach. I get the feeling that he's great at what he does, because I've read about his achievements on the internet. (Everything we read on the internet is true, right? Joke.) Well, for years, my relative had been a community college coach who has been interested to become a minor league batting coach and then eventually work his way up to being a major league batting coach. Over two years, he had interviews with four different minor league baseball teams and each time he came away empty. Frustrated, he finally decided to go back to the people he interviewed with and find out why they hadn't hired him and what the differences were between him and the persons they hired. The first two organizations he called were forthcoming enough to tell him that they were concerned with whether he would be able to work well with the Latin American players, as he did not speak Spanish. For those of you that don't know, there are a large percentage of Latin American players in the US minor and major baseball leagues and not all of them speak or understand English proficiently. So, armed with this information, my relative took it upon himself to take some accelerated Spanish classes. Sure enough, by the time the next season came around, he was very competent at speaking Spanish. He applied for a job as a minor league batting coach and he was hired. A couple lessons can be learned from his experience. First, he solicited feedback on why he'd been previously rejected. Second, he analyzed that information and determined that he probably wasn't winning those jobs because he didn't speak Spanish, even though that was never advertised as a requirement for the

## Job Interview Preparation

job. Third, he realized that he could change that deficiency and took some Spanish courses.

4) Promise to learn something from your rejection. It's no secret that we can learn a lot from our failures. And if we don't learn from our failures, we'll keep repeating them. If you've been rejected for a job, take it upon yourself to analyze what you could have done better and learn from it. Otherwise, all of the time and effort you spent preparing for that interview will surely go to waste. Try to take something valuable away from each rejection.

5) Refine your search. With the interview for the job you didn't get, was there anything you didn't like about the jobs or the companies you interviewed with? Rejection aside, maybe you discovered some things about the job or the company that weren't as great as you thought they would be. If so, you might use this information to refine your search. As an example, if someone applies for an accounting management job and they realize from the interview that the job requires a lot more managing of people that it does accounting. And the person who applied for this job really isn't interested much in managing people. He would prefer more to be involved in just the accounting aspects of an accounting job. With that self-analysis, he can refine his future searches to accounting jobs that do not include management responsibilities.

6) Focus on the process, not the outcome. My clients will tell you that I harp on the idea that, in looking for a job, they need to focus on the process of going about getting a job

and preparing and interviewing well instead of the outcome. Interviewing is a process and you won't be able to control the outcome of who is chosen for the job. However, if you can continue to fine tune the methods you are using to get and prepare for the interviews and continue to analyze and refine the way you're interviewing, you'll give yourself the best chance to manipulate the outcome. So, focus on the process and not the outcome.

# **Conclusion**

So, there you have it. Now that you've read this book, you have the tools to go out and get the interviews you want. You also have some tips and techniques which should help you interview more successfully, be your best self, and land the job you really want.

We've discussed a variety of topics you can use in increase your chances of getting the job. You can get more interviews by using the tips I've given you to build a better resume. You can position yourself above other candidates by writing cover letters that will grab the reader and tell the interviewer why you are someone who is a formidable candidate who they have to interview.

We've discussed how to dress for an interview, how to overcome nervousness and anxiety. We've discussed the importance of doing your homework and researching the company you're interviewing with, so you can avoid the "So, what do you all do here?" question to start your interview. You should also have a better handle on how to navigate difficult questions in an interview and you now know what questions to ask during an interview. You know how to handle questions that catch you off-guard. With the right body language and an air of confidence, you'll be able to stand out and make a killer first impression. You now know what prospective employers want to hear and you know things they don't want to hear. And you know how to follow up after a job interview. If you're fortunate enough to become the leading candidate, you'll know how to negotiate to get the optimum salary. You'll also know what needs to happen after you accept an offer.

Bottom line, you now have the tools in your toolbox to score and ace interviews.

## Job Interview Preparation

As I've mentioned before, the job interview process is a competition. You'll be competing against other candidates who have the same goal as you do—to get the job. If you're going to have a chance, you'll have to find a way to stand out from these other candidates. You're going to have to tweak and fine-tune your interview process. Although I've known people who have maintained that they had a perfect interview, but didn't get the job, I've always encouraged those people to continue to go back and analyze their process. Did they really do everything right? Isn't there something they could have improved upon?

Interviewing for a job can be a frustrating process, mostly because it includes some elements that are beyond your control. With the candidates who have felt that they've done everything right throughout the interview process, but still haven't landed the job, I tell them the same thing I'll tell you: In interviewing for jobs, it's important for you to focus on the process of getting the job, not the outcome. You can control what you do in your efforts to get the job, but you can't control whether you get the job. Unfortunately, that's beyond your control. So again, with those things in mind, focus on the process, not the outcome. If you can do that, I assure you that you'll have more success in getting interviews and you'll increase your chances of landing the job.

If you don't get a job, for whatever reason, don't hang your head. If you can learn from your past rejections, those rejections will ultimately help you improve your process. Yes, I have clients who tell me that they're tired of learning from their mistakes. That being said, I always remind them that searching for a new job is often a numbers game. It's a process, not an event. The more and the quicker you can fine-tune your process, the quicker you'll be able to land that new job.

You've now spent some of your valuable time in reading this book. I'm hoping that you'll now take the time to implement immediately some of the tips and techniques I've given you. With many self-help or "how to" books such as this one, readers make the mistake of not resolving to make changes immediately. They'll resolve to make changes someday, whenever they get around to it. Unfortunately, most of those people never get around to it. That's why I encourage you to make changes and change your process immediately. If you are willing to do that, you'll surely enhance your chances of getting the job you want. Although I can't guarantee that you'll get every job you apply for, I can say that if you use the tools I've provided, you'll be able to be your best self in trying to get interviews and you'll have a much better chance to succeed in the interviews you have.

So, let's get after it!

Wishing you more interviews and more interview success. Happy hunting!

# CONVERSATION SKILLS 2.0 TALK TO ANYONE AND DEVELOP MAGNETIC CHARISMA

*Discover Cutting-Edge Methods to Enhance Your Communication Skills in Just 7 Days, Even If You're Shy or Introverted*

# Table of Contents

Introduction ................................................................... **108**

**Chapter 1 - Establishing Likability** ................................... **111**
    The Confirmation Bias ............................................... 111
    The Qualities & Behaviors that Make You Instantly Likable ..... 112
    What Determines Likable Behavior? ........................... 116
    The Seven Bad Habits that are Making You Unlikable ........ 117

**Chapter 2 - The Basics of Good Conversation** ............ **121**
    How to Make Great First Impressions ......................... 121
    Win at Small Talk with the ARE Model ...................... 124
    Three Essential Ways to Get Along with Anyone You Meet ..... 125
    Six Tips for Resisting Shyness and a Lack of Confidence ......... 128

**Chapter 3 - Igniting Exceptional Interactions** ............. **132**
    Conversation Topics & Tips for Every Possible Scenario ......... 132
    The Worst Mistakes You Can Make in a Conversation ............. 136
    Ideas to Steer Clear of Boring Conversations ..................... 141
    Three General Rules for Sparking an Interesting Conversation . 143

**Chapter 4 - Cultivating Charisma and Magnetism** ..... **145**
    The Thirteen Secrets to Developing a Magnetic Personality ...... 145
    All You Need to Know About the Trifecta of Charm ............... 151
    Three Steps to Becoming a More Interesting Person ............. 156

**Chapter 5 - Knowing Your Audience** .......................... **159**
    Microexpressions ....................................................... 159
    The Six Types of Communicators & How to Win Them Over .. 161
    Conversation Tips for Special Audiences ......................... 165

**Chapter 6 - Building Deep Connections** ..................... **168**

Conversation Tricks to Instantly Build Rapport with Someone . 168
How to Form Meaningful Relationships ..................................... 170
The Habits of Emotionally Intelligent People ........................... 172
Why Self-Compassion is Important for Healthy Relationships.. 175

**Chapter 7 - Difficult Situations & Social Blunders ..................... 177**
How to talk your way out of difficult or awkward situations ..... 177
Coping with Difficult Personalities ........................................... 181
When is it okay to lie? ............................................................... 186

**Chapter 8 - Using Conversation to Get What You Want .......... 188**
Subtle ways of showing dominance ............................................ 188
Persuasion Techniques for all Situations ................................... 190
Three Tricks to Seduce Someone through Conversation ........... 193
Six Highly Effective Tips for Successful Negotiations .............. 196

**Conclusion ...................................................................................... 199**

## Job Interview Preparation

© Copyright 2019 by _____ - All rights reserved.

The following book is reproduced below with the goal of providing information that is as accurate and reliable as possible. Regardless, purchasing this book can be seen as consent to the fact that both the publisher and the author of this book are in no way experts on the topics discussed within and that any recommendations or suggestions that are made herein are for entertainment purposes only. Professionals should be consulted as needed prior to undertaking any of the action endorsed herein.

This declaration is deemed fair and valid by both the American Bar Association and the Committee of Publishers Association and is legally binding throughout the United States.

Furthermore, the transmission, duplication, or reproduction of any of the following work including specific information will be considered an illegal act irrespective of if it is done electronically or in print. This extends to creating a secondary or tertiary copy of the work or a recorded copy and is only allowed with the express written consent from the Publisher. All additional rights reserved.

The information in the following pages is broadly considered a truthful and accurate account of facts and as such, any inattention, use, or misuse of the information in question by the reader will render any resulting actions solely under their purview. There are no scenarios in which the publisher or the original author of this work can be in any fashion deemed liable for any hardship or damages that may befall them after undertaking information described herein.

Additionally, the information in the following pages is intended only for informational purposes and should thus be thought of as universal. As befitting its nature, it is presented without assurance regarding its prolonged validity or interim quality. Trademarks that are mentioned are done without written consent and can in no way be considered an endorsement from the trademark holder.

# **Introduction**

I know the real reason you opened this book: you're desperate to see change in your day-to-day life. You're bored of lackluster social interactions, a dead-end career and you're disappointed by your strained or unfulfilling relationships. You know it can get better - you've seen other people develop the kind of relationships you desire - and you want to own that kind of social influence now.

This may surprise you, but you're not the only one who feels this way. Leagues of people across the world dream of these same changes and, like you, they have a hunch that the solution lies in amping-up their social abilities. Like you, they want to be a conversational master.

But the good news is, you're already one step ahead of them.

Why? It's simple. You've taken the first step. You've opened this book. You're about to commit to greater achievements and more powerful relationships – and that makes you a tad smarter than the rest. Congratulations on getting a little closer to your goals.

Perhaps you're awkward and shy. Perhaps, you constantly feel overpowered in social settings, like your presence doesn't matter. You never know the right thing to say and it feels like you're always one beat behind the rest.

Or perhaps, you're not socially awkward at all, you simply want to wield more influence over your peers and make a stronger impact on everyone you meet. You've seen the way some people get what they want using only their words, and you want to experience what it's like. I'll tell you now, this experience can be yours with some practice and expert wisdom. It's not as difficult as it looks, you just need the right training.

Whatever stage you're at, whether you're a timid wallflower or a fairly confident conversationalist, this book will take you to the same destination: the top of your communication game. This book will show you the entire spectrum, from the very basics of good conversation to the advanced tools of persuasion and influence. We'll break down language, behavior, and personality into their digestible parts - and you'll achieve mastery over them all. You'll learn how to befriend, seduce, and resolve conflict with only the magic of communication. And by the end of your training, you'll know how to navigate nearly every situation known to man. From the difficult, strained scenarios to the intimate and deep connections.

Make no mistake, these skills will shake the foundation of your entire life. After all, the quality of our relationships is directly influenced by how well or how badly we communicate. It can mean the difference between constant fighting and empowering conversation. Or the difference between a dull interaction and smooth-talking your way into a life-changing opportunity. Our only warning? We hope you're ready for these newfound abilities.

You see, communication is the closest thing to magic that exists. Once you master tone, language, timing, and a few other essential factors, you can produce any desired effect. The human mind is malleable, and except for the occasional idiosyncrasy, human needs are pretty easy to anticipate. Understanding them is the key to forming successful social strategies. You'll soon learn all about this.

I developed these advanced skills the hard way: through trial and error, through falling prey to the tactics of masters, and getting to know every personality type imaginable, no matter how aggravating. I studied the methods of a diverse range of people and learned from their mistakes as well as their successes. I said and did the wrong thing – but then I learned to say the right thing. And I perfected the right thing. I discovered when the right thing works best, when it doesn't work at all and when the right thing must give way to a better thing. I observed every move, every subtlety. And then I did extensive research to expand on what I already knew. I dissected the powerful areas of communication most people overlook; I will teach you to never overlook them again and how to use them to your fullest advantage.

# Job Interview Preparation

I have watched fragile nobodies evolve into masters of persuasion with a presence that cannot be ignored. I am often thanked by people who have used my advice, with claims that it transformed their personal relationships, and helped them create new, more meaningful ones, as well. But it's no surprise that these benefits arise. Perfecting the art of conversation is synonymous with perfecting one's ability to live in tandem with other human beings. The people I've helped have become experts at both. I will be sharing these same secrets with you, very shortly.

With my help and expertise, you'll move past crippling shyness, dullness, and all breeds of social ineptitude. Instead, you'll spark fascinating interactions, deep connections and develop all the skills necessary to own every room you enter. You won't just open doors to new opportunities; you'll charm those doors right off their hinges. My guides will run the gamut, from seducing romantic interests to negotiating a better deal, children, difficult personalities, and more. You will need no other communication guide again. Consider this your conversation bible.

You've made that vital first step – now don't make the common mistake of ending the journey here. Remember this important fact: complacency is the silent killer of all potential. What doors are you allowing to shut while you sit idly?

As you reveal this book's next chapter, so shall you unveil *your* new chapter. Welcome to the only communication guide you'll ever need.

# Chapter 1 - Establishing Likability

Imagine this: a man saunters into the party you're attending. He's dressed exceptionally well in a crisp, button-down shirt, smart casual pants, and polished leather shoes. He makes eye contact with everyone in the room for a brief moment, smiling occasionally, and gesturing a friendly hello to someone he recognizes. His body is open towards the room, and he's even nodding his head slightly to the rhythm of the music playing in the background. The woman you're talking to - your new acquaintance, Claire - notices him. She waves and beams, and he does the same. He looks between you both, surveying the situation, and then he comes over slowly, ready to introduce himself with a warm smile.

Before he's even said a word, this man has established himself as a likable person. There's a high likelihood that you already feel comfortable letting him join your conversation. You may even feel the desire to get to know him and consider him as a potential friend. It's true that you don't really know who he is, and it's possible he could be the opposite of what you expect – but the point is, you want to find out. And because he's displayed likable behavior, he's already at an advantage.

## The Confirmation Bias

When we have a preexisting idea or belief, we tend to only notice factors that can confirm our assumptions. This idea forms the crux of the confirmation bias. In other words, you see what you want to see to confirm your initial judgment was correct. Humans enjoy being right. And so we absorb information selectively to prove our point, not disprove it.

How does this play into our scenario with the likable man? Let's say you finally speak to him, and he mistakenly assumes he's met you before and calls you by the wrong name. This would be a social flub on his part, but if you'd already established that you think he's likable, you'd probably let it slide easily. In fact, you'd probably think, "Oh, it's a simple mistake. It happens sometimes and you can't help it. I'm sure he meets a lot of people." You'd then forget it and instead choose to remember how kind he was when he apologized.

But consider this other scenario: let's say, it was a different man, and he walked into the room with a scowl and a tight jaw. When he looked around the room, his eyes lingered a bit too long and inappropriately on a good-looking woman, and when he noticed your friend, he raised his eyebrows and didn't smile. If the same occurrence happened where he called you by the wrong name, you probably wouldn't be so forgiving. You'd maybe think, "Clearly he doesn't really respect people." You would choose to remember the mistake he made, and even if he apologized, chances are you'd be harder to win over.

In both scenarios, you're only looking to confirm what you already believe – but you could be completely wrong about both assumptions. The first man could turn out to be an arrogant narcissist and the second man could turn out to be intelligent and kind, just very socially awkward. The problem is, we'd only know for sure if we sat down and got to know these men on a deeper level. But most social interactions don't grant us that much time and chances are, you've already decided you don't want to get to know the unlikable man.

This is why we must emphasize likable behavior. People are assessing whether they like or don't like you, and whether they want to get to know you or not, as soon as you walk in the room. And this will greatly influence all proceeding interactions. You may have a great personality, but no one will ever know about it if your behavior comes across as cold, awkward, or uninviting. Start off on the right foot and send positive signals.

## The Qualities & Behaviors that Make You Instantly Likable

1. **An Impressive Appearance**

Contrary to popular belief, an impressive appearance doesn't just consist of good looks or expensive clothing. It encompasses everything about the way we carry and present ourselves to the world. It includes:

- The way you dress

Dressing well does not always mean formal. In fact, a necessary part of dressing well is making sure you've dressed appropriately for the occasion. If someone arrives at a low-key social gathering in a sharp suit for no reason, they may be perceived as pretentious. Conversely, if it's a formal event and you attend wearing sneakers, you'll be seen as sloppy and not taking it seriously.

People who dress sharply for every occasion (this means fitted, neat, and appropriate clothing) will always command more respect than someone who doesn't care at all about what they're wearing. Why? Not only does it send the message that you're intelligent and competent, it also tells people, "I am extremely socially aware and I have the means to take care of myself."

- The way you speak

Do you mumble or slur your words? Do you laugh nervously between sentences? Or do you enunciate and speak at just the right pace? The way you speak is a reflection of many important attributes. It will determine greatly how people perceive you and better yet, the way others will choose to interact with you. If your voice is too soft and slow, you will get overpowered. Studies have shown that those who display quiet voices give off the impression of being weak and inexperienced. At the opposite end, however, a voice that is high-pitched and loud is perceived to be unreliable, arrogant, and impatient. The ideal voice is firm, well-defined, and at a medium pace and volume. Even if you're saying a simple greeting, project the voice that suits the message you want to send.

## 2. Open and Interested Body Language

Your gestures and stances are sending messages as well. You may not be aware of it, but every person who encounters you will respond to the positioning of your body. To enhance your likability, it's imperative that you display a sense of openness.

- <u>Turn towards the person you're speaking to</u>

Your face may be angled towards your conversation partner, but what about the rest of your body? When you're turned away, your body language could be interpreted as uninterested or nervous. Facing them squarely, however, will make you appear invested and interested in the conversation. This, in turn, will make people more inclined to engage with you.

- <u>Gesture with your hands or let your arms hang loose</u>

People tend to overlook what their arms are doing when they're conversing, but this is another tell-tale sign of how a person feels. Arms that are tight and locked give the impression of someone insecure or rigid. To appear more likable, let them hang loose and if you can, gesture as you speak. People tend to respond well to someone who is expressive with their hands. This will demonstrate that you're comfortable, confident and enthusiastic about the situation at hand.

- <u>Mirror your conversation partner's behavior</u>

Humans have a deep need to make connection with someone else. An effective way to ignite feelings of connection is to mimic someone's behavior in conversation. When they say something and smile, try smiling too. If they take a sip of their drink, you should as well. This will make the other party feel that you're in alignment with them, like you're on the same page. However, for mirroring to work successfully, it's important that you don't do it for the entire length of the conversation as this will seem unnatural and the other person will likely notice. Psychologists also advise not mirroring right away. If a conversation has not had time to find its rhythm, any conscious mimicry will be seen as such.

- Loose and upright posture

We all know that standing straighter conveys a more appealing impression, but that's not all there is to it. Our posture must also be fairly loose, as this tells people we're welcoming and comfortable. People who stand straight and rigidly tend to seem unapproachable and sometimes even severe.

## 3. Looking Happy to Be There

When a person looks happy to be where they are, they look comfortable and safe to be around. When we encounter someone who appears this way, we instinctively feel comfortable too, and we sense that their company must be pleasant. This is similar to displaying open body language, but not entirely the same. Open body language will say we're available, but a happy and pleasant aura will actually send the invitation.

- Smiling just the right amount

The most recognizable signal for happiness is the smile, and it's an easy way to convey your pleasure. Keep a relaxed smile on your face and you'll find that more people start interacting with you. Smile at the appropriate intervals when someone is telling a story and smile when you see someone that you know. Just be careful to not grin too much or too widely if it's not entirely genuine. A fake smile can be alarming and creepy, and may produce an adverse effect.

- Make sure your neutral expression is relaxed and pleasant

Many of us lose control of our neutral expressions. We think we look perfectly normal, but other people might still think we're unapproachable. Have you ever seen someone with Resting Bitch Face (RBF)? Exactly. Stay aware of what your neutral expression is. Even if you're just wandering over to the snack table to grab more finger food, keep your expression relaxed, with the corners of your mouth upturned ever so slightly. This is not a full on smile, but it conveys the message that you're happy to be there.

## What Determines Likable Behavior?

Likable behavior is not made up of a random set of traits and actions, they can all be drawn down to the same basic needs. We search for basic assurances in every single person we encounter and this will determine how positively we respond to them as well as how likely we are to seek their company again. If you keep your conversation partners' three basic needs in mind, you may find yourself displaying likable behavior naturally.

- Safety

You may not realize this, but a number of qualities we search for, such as approachability and trustworthiness, can all be attributed to our desire for safety. The basic animal nature in us all wants to ensure that we'll receive no threats to our well-being. It's not just about our physical safety, but our sense of self as we know it. We want to avoid emotional and mental threats, just as we want to avoid a physical threat. When a person displays approachability or trustworthiness, they are essentially saying 'You're safe around me.' Once our brains pick up this signal, we relax and open ourselves to the possibility of connection.

- Significance

Once we establish we're safe, we soften to the idea of connecting, but we're not there immediately. We also want to feel significant and important on some level. It's not enough that a person is approachable. If they aren't really listening to what we're saying, or they're always looking over our shoulder cause they are waiting for an opportunity to talk to someone else, chances are we won't be entirely impressed. Even if someone is smiling and acting very kind, we can always sense when our presence is truly valued and desired. Naturally, we want to be where we are appreciated.

- Expansion

A new acquaintance has successfully made us feel comfortable and significant in their presence – but there's still something missing. The cherry on top of the cake is expansion and an opportunity for growth. The desire to evolve and become better than we are is a natural human need. The solution to this need can take many forms, but it all comes down to a feeling of excitement and positive challenge.

When we meet someone that entertains us and stimulates us intellectually, our need for mental and emotional expansion is fulfilled. This need also encompasses humor since what we find truly funny, subconsciously tickles our intellect. We've all encountered jokes that we consider "too dumb" or jokes we just "don't get."

This is the hardest need to take care of since personal taste can play a large role here. It is also important to note that people who can take care of each other's needs for expansion are usually from roughly the same IQ level. What one person finds interesting can be extremely boring or confusing to another person.

## The Seven Bad Habits that are Making You Unlikable

Remember the unlikable guy from earlier? He's displaying a myriad of social turn-offs that are sending the wrong messages.

But do you want to know a terrifying thought? You, too, have definitely made some of those mistakes before. In fact, you might even make them to this day. Let's examine some classic and lesser known social mistakes, so you can start becoming more likable right now.

1. **Constantly on the Phone**

No one should feel bad for glancing at their phone or typing a quick text message, but in this modern day and age, such restraint is rare. If you have your phone out constantly, and are seen scrolling through social media while in the company of other people, you're going to leave a bad impression. Being absorbed by your device when other people expect you to stay present is seen as extremely rude. Would you start reading a book in the middle of a social gathering? Any decent person wouldn't, and this is not much different to frequent phone distractions. Save this behavior for when you're by yourself or at a very casual hang-out.

If you're expecting a call or trying to resolve something important via text, do so in another room. Or alternatively, apologize to the people you're with and explain how you're dealing with an important matter. This advice also applies to loud phone conversations in public. Find another room or lower your voice.

### 2. Slouching or Slumping in Your Seat

Unless you're at your best friend's house for a casual hang-out, slouching or slumping in your seat sends the signal that you're either lazy or submissive. To people you don't know, it can even convey a complete lack of interest in what they're saying. By slouching or slumping, you make your body appear smaller, and instinctively we interpret this as a lack of confidence and power.

### 3. Inappropriate or Lack of Eye Contact

Watching what someone does with their eyes is a great way to get a good read on them. Are they displaying judgment by looking everyone up and down? Are they being misogynistic by staring at women inappropriately? Or are they awkward and standoffish, making no eye contact at all? All of the above are examples of what can turn us off a new acquaintance. Avoid making those mistakes.

### 4. Bad Hygiene

When someone smells bad or looks like they haven't washed themselves in days, they're saying, "I can't take care of myself." As intelligent animals who are interested in self-preservation, we are wired to be repelled by something that we think is dirty. Subconsciously we associate it with breeding grounds for organisms and diseases that could threaten our well-being. Even if we know a person isn't diseased, the self-preserving animal in us has learned to have this reaction to potentially unsanitary situations, objects, or people.

Of course, no one stops caring for a friend or loved one because they have bad hygiene, but it is the reason we have the urge to hold our nose and sit further away from them. These reactions are not conducive to positive social interactions.

This reflex is hardwired into us in the same way we can't help but blink and produce tears when a foreign particle gets into our eyes. These are ways the living body has learned to cope with potential threats.

For this reason, most people (except for those who already live in unsanitary conditions) are repelled by bad hygiene. While it's perfectly normal to have a sweaty day now and then, where you may not smell as fresh as you usually do, consistent grime will make it difficult for you to charm anyone.

### 5. Not Participating in Conversations

Being mysterious is one thing, but if you are always seen staying completely silent in social settings, this can make you seem unfriendly or even dim-witted. When reserved people are in the presence of their outgoing friends, it comes naturally to let the talkers do the talking, but they should resist this urge. Even if it's just a one-liner or a question here and there, make sure you are contributing something to every conversation you're involved in. It's really quite simple: if you don't offer anything, you look like you have nothing to offer.

### 6. Not Dressing Appropriately

Remember what we said about dressing well for every occasion? Not everyone has a great sense of style, and that's okay, but at the very least, you must make sure you dress appropriately. This applies to men and women. Save your skimpy skirts and surfer tank tops for parties with your good friends, but never wear them to formal events or first-time meetings with your significant other's parents. Keep this in mind: always dress in alignment with the message you want to send to the room.

### 7. Not Respecting Personal Space

Personal space is more than just getting in someone's way or touching someone you don't know well. It encompasses behavior like cutting in front of a stranger in line, going through someone's belongings without permission, or entering someone's bedroom, office, or house without knocking first. Even actions that are intended to be friendly, like forcibly hugging someone you don't know, can be experienced as a violation of personal space. It depends on whether you were given verbal or nonverbal consent to enter someone's space or touch their property (and this includes their body).

Always respect the privacy of others, and their right to refuse physical contact. Anyone who witnesses such an invasion will see you as disrespectful and socially inept.

Never lose track of the way you present yourself to the world, whether physically or behaviorally. A conversation is far more than our verbal communications; it's also about what we say with our actions and responses. To truly master conversation skills, you must conquer the art of likable behavior.

# Chapter 2 - The Basics of Good Conversation

You've learned how to behave in public, but the journey is far from over. As soon as you open your mouth to enter a conversation, you're in a different arena and a new set of skills comes into play. Our image is one thing, but as soon as this phase of communication begins, people finally get to see how that image stacks up against what we say and how we say it. Are we all that we portray ourselves to be? Are we as impressive as the words on our resume? Are we as classy as the way we dress?

## How to Make Great First Impressions

You may think that short interactions are easier to pull off, but that could not be less true. Unlike sit-down chats or long conversations, you have a shorter amount of time to win the other party over. If you behave awkwardly or say something you shouldn't have, before you know it time's up, and that's how they'll remember you from now onwards. You have one try and then it's over until the next meeting, if it even exists.

Learning to master first impressions and small talk are crucial for many life-shaping events. A potential new employer doesn't have time or the interest to get to know you in depth, you need to charm him in a short amount of time. And the same rule applies to that cute boy or girl you run into sometimes. You need to make a good impression before you get that date.

To turn that one-time encounter into something more, here are some essential tips:

- **Butter up your introduction**

Don't just say 'My name is Peter,' say 'My name is Peter, it's really nice to meet you.' You'd be surprised by how simple a sentence can

## Job Interview Preparation

take your first impression up a few notches. This will immediately warm any new person to you, as you've successfully made them feel important, interesting, and like you want to continue being around them. We've established that humans enjoy feeling safe and significant; this is an easy, simple way to tick both those boxes immediately.

- **Learn how to give a good handshake**

Many potential employers and professional connections pay attention to the way you shake their hand. Keep in mind these three major factors: the strength of your grip, the duration, and the positioning of your hand.

The perfect handshake is not too soft, not too tight, but perfectly firm. You should shake their hand for two to three pumps, for no more than three seconds, but ideally two seconds. During the handshake, your arm should also be perfectly vertical. Never show the underside of your wrist or the top of your forearm, as this shows submission or dominance respectively.

Please note that if you shake hands with an individual who puts your hand on the bottom, with your wrist exposed, this means they are making a power play. If they pull you towards them as they shake your hand, they are also performing a power move. These are classic signs of exerting dominance. We don't advise making these power plays on other people, unless you are prepared for some tension.

- **Be considerate**

There's a good reason this encounter is brief. Perhaps you're talking to someone while they're at work, between meetings, or at a crowded social event. Whatever the scenario, be considerate of other peoples' time and attention. Consider the circumstances and question at what point you might become an intrusion. Are you trying to talk to someone while they're working? Or perhaps they're on their short lunch break and you're holding them up in the office corridor? Don't insist on holding a person's attention for a long time, when you know you're not the only reason they're there.

- **Make eye contact**

During quick encounters, many people shy away from eye contact. Whether it's due to social awkwardness or because you've been caught by surprise, resist the urge to let this discomfort be seen. Make sufficient eye contact with the person you're speaking with, but also resist the urge to stare. Look directly at them as they speak. For one-on-one conversations, you should break eye contact every 7-10 seconds. For group settings, however, try and break eye contact between 4-6 seconds.

- **Ask a question to show you're interested**

It's a quick chat, sure, but it's fine to shoot off a question as long as it's easy to answer and they aren't in a rush to get anywhere. This shows that you're interested and curious about them, since you chose to ask a question when you didn't have to. This is even more important for job interviews since employers expect questions, and will even judge prospective employees based on the questions they ask. Whatever the situation, make sure the questions you ask during brief encounters are not too personal or time-consuming.

- **Don't be *too* honest when you answer the question "How are you?"**

There are some individuals with which we *can* be honest about how we're doing – but they're all people we already know well, in which case, we are long past the stage of worrying about first-impressions. With the rest, however, it's best to keep it light and positive. Even if you're going through a difficult period in your life, understate it in a way that the other person doesn't suddenly feel they have to ask what's wrong and console you. Say something like, "I've been better, but I'm sure things will look up soon." Often when people ask you how you are, they're doing so out of politeness and good social decorum. Save your long, honest answers for your good friends and family. And always remember to ask the other person the same question!

- **Use environmental triggers**

If you can't think of a single thing to say, look around you. There's material everywhere! If you're running into someone at a grocery store, you could ask if they shop there often. If the encounter takes place at the train station, you could share where you're going and ask where they're headed as well. If the person in question is wearing something particularly striking, compliment them! Look around you in the moment and you'll realize there's a lot to talk about.

- **Give an uplifting goodbye**

Sometimes you get lucky and the person you've run into is someone you want to see again soon. You may make plans and part with a happy, "See you on Tuesday!" Most of the time, however, you're probably running into someone you don't care to see again, or someone you're not sure you'll see again, such as a prospective employer. To make the best impression, send them off with some positive and uplifting parting words. Tell them "Have a great day!" or give them well wishes in regards to what they've shared with you. For example, "Good luck with your marathon!" or "Have a great time at dinner!"

## Win at Small Talk with the ARE Model

If you want a simple, easy formula for good small talk, this section is for you. Carol Fleming, a communications expert and coach, created a three-point method for helping individuals get better at small-talk. This plan works on shy and confident folks alike. ARE stands for:

- **Anchor** – To begin, find something that you are your conversation partner both have in common in the current moment. Fleming describes this as your "shared reality." Look around and see what you notice. It could be anything from the food being served or someone in an outrageous outfit that you can both see. Anchoring involves choosing a focus and stating the observation. For example, let's say you're making small talk at a fancy party. You tell a new acquaintance: "These appetizers are delicious."

- **Reveal** – Then comes something about you. Share a slightly personal tidbit that's relevant to the topic you've just brought up. It doesn't have to be complicated or mind-blowing. This is just to establish the dynamic of sharing with each other. You could say, "I wish I could make something like this, but I'm just not very skilled in the kitchen."

- **Encourage** – Finally, you give your acquaintance an opening to respond. Focus on being friendly and encouraging so that they share information about themselves with you. This should take the form of a question. An idea is: "Are you a good cook? You look like someone with a lot of hidden talents!"

Whenever you're feeling nervous or more unsteady than usual, remember this formula to get yourself back into the small-talk groove. Don't shy away from small talk. It's the precursor to a long, engaging conversation with a potential new friend or professional connection. It is the first step that leads to all other steps. Keep these tools in mind to start winning at small talk.

## Three Essential Ways to Get Along with Anyone You Meet

We all know someone with seemingly irresistible charm; someone who's liked by everyone they meet, no matter the personality type and no matter the circumstance. The trick to getting along with others is not rocket science, but it does require a big mental and behavioral shift. We might have already displayed likable behavior, earning the interest of a new conversation partner, but now we need to know how to sustain this interest. Now that someone has given us the chance to get to know them, we need a new set of skills to create conversational harmony.

## 1. Show Genuine Interest in Others

It seems simple, doesn't it? And yet you'd be surprised by how many fail this basic step. Showing genuine interest requires more than just nodding and smiling. Remember the basic social need for significance? The person you're conversing with must feel that you care about what they're saying and who they are. We all want to feel as though we are valued and appreciated. These behaviors can demonstrate genuine interest:

- Ask questions. Get to know the person you're conversing with better, but make sure to do so in a way that is not interrogative, and steer clear of questions that are too personal unless you know them well. If they are telling you about an activity they enjoy, ask them why they like it, or when they started.

- Pay attention. When someone is talking, stay present and listen to what they're saying. Most people can sense when the person they're talking to has zoned out of the conversation, and this is a major social turn off. Why would you want to talk to someone who isn't listening? You wouldn't. If someone is telling a story, try to paint a mental picture with the details they're giving you. A good trick is to imagine what they're saying as a movie.

- Show enthusiasm. When someone talks to you, don't just nod and blink like a fool. Smile, look receptive, and when they share new information with you, show enthusiasm. When necessary, respond with phrases like, "Wow, that's very interesting!" or "How wonderful. That's great to hear." People always respond well to enthusiastic positivity.

## 2. Be Kind

People who display kindness are pleasant to be around: that's a fact. We instinctively feel safe around them and develop trust for them. An act or word of kindness can easily brighten up a day, and it's an important step to getting along with someone. You'll be hard pressed to find someone who isn't won over by kindness. Here are some ideas for showing your nice side:

- Display good manners. That's right, everything your parents taught you about saying please and thank you, holding open the door, respecting personal space, and all the rest, are all valuable social skills. Manners display consideration for other people. The reason we are taught this when we are young is because this is the most basic form of human kindness. Display good manners and you'll start off on the right foot.

- Empathize. This doesn't mean you have to listen to someone's problems and hold their hand; we can always empathize, even over small matters. Perhaps, you're at a formal dinner and someone's food gets forgotten. Say something like, "I'm so sorry you have to wait. It's always annoying when food doesn't arrive on time." It's simple, but filled with empathy. The other person will immediately feel like you care about them, and will be highly receptive to anything else you might say.

## 3. Open Up

Remember our need for expansion? It's not enough to be kind and receptive, we should also show our conversation partners that we have something to offer them. We do this by opening up, talking about ourselves, and responding to what they say in a thoughtful, informative or entertaining manner.

- Share your experiences. The best part of this is it can be anything that delights you to share. The only requirements are that it is appropriate and doesn't dominate the entire conversation for an extended period of time. You can share anything, from a funny encounter you had that day to a fascinating experience you had abroad. Keep it interesting and leave out the unnecessary details. When we share stories with others, it allows them to get to know us and invites them to see what is interesting about us.

- Share an interesting thought, feeling, or observation. If you don't have any relevant experiences to share, or you simply can't think of anything, then try to respond to your current surroundings or the conversation at hand. Ideally, it would be something that reflects your personal taste or an opinion you hold. They want to get to know you, remember?

## Six Tips for Resisting Shyness and a Lack of Confidence

Some of you can't help it – you're shy, and that's just the way you are. You're more wary of people, and you've never understood how chatterboxes can so freely interact with others they don't know. Even if you have the desire to socialize, you end up not contributing very much to the conversation. Sometimes this is because you have social anxiety and a lack of confidence, and other times, it's just because you're more reserved than the average person.

There's nothing wrong with being shy or reserved, but you'll definitely encounter situations in your life where you'll need to talk more than you're comfortable with. Perhaps you're talking to a prospective employer, or maybe you're meeting a significant other's parents for the first time. To safeguard against awkward moments and silences, keep these tips in mind:

# Job Interview Preparation

## 1. Prepare beforehand

If you're nervous about an upcoming social interaction, there's nothing wrong with preparing for it in advance. Think of interesting stories to tell, and perhaps even practice the way you want to tell them. If you're feeling confident, prepare some jokes. Make sure you know them well but try not to over-rehease, or they won't sound natural.

If you already know about potential conversation topics that the other person will bring up, it's also a great idea to think of how you will respond. For example, if you're about to spend time with someone who recently did a lot of traveling, think of an interesting travel experience that you've had, and practice telling the story in an amusing way. Use what you know about the people you're spending time with to come up with great conversation topics and stories.

If you're about to meet your significant other's parents for the first time, and you know they'll ask you about your career or where you grew up, think of engaging and relevant stories that you can share with them. To be extra prepared, come up with a list of questions to ask whenever there is a lull in the conversation.

Planned interactions can turn out extremely well, and the best part is, you'll feel a lot more confident afterwards.

## 2. Focus away from yourself

If you dread being the center of attention, this is a tip for you. There are many ways to direct the spotlight onto someone else. One sure way is to ask lots of questions. Instead of staying silent, try to learn about someone else. This will reflect upon you positively as you'll also appear curious and interested, two qualities that people tend to be drawn to. You won't have to feel vulnerable, and yet you're still participating in the conversation.

To keep attention off yourself for as long as possible, make sure to ask open-ended questions, not just something that can be answered with a 'yes' or 'no.' If you meet someone from a foreign place, ask them what it's like where they are from, and if you're speaking with a work acquaintance, ask them what they like to do on the weekends. To successfully avoid the spotlight, think of more questions to keep the conversation evolving. Otherwise, the other person will likely ask "How about you?" if silence presents itself.

### 3. Focus on connecting, not impressing

During moments of anxiety, people tend to forget that it's more important to connect than it is to impress. If you focus on impressing, you'll most likely come across as trying too hard and making all the wrong moves. People can sense when someone is actively trying to impress, and this tends to produce a negative reaction. What you should focus on is genuine connection. Get to know the other person, empathize with them, and don't be afraid to give them a genuine compliment. Instead of thinking about all the ways you can show off, really listen to what they're saying and respond in a thoughtful manner. Try to also discover your common interests.

### 4. Don't be someone you're not

Shy people should never forget this fact. In the pursuit of better conversation skills, it can be easy to feel like you're trying to be someone else, but it's important to remember it's not like that at all. It's not about giving yourself qualities that you don't have, it's about developing enough confidence to share the qualities you possess with other people. Shy people should never feel the need to pretend they're extroverted or gregarious people. It's about getting used to including your great qualities and interesting experiences in the wider conversation.

There are many ways that people pretend to be someone they are not. Sometimes this manifests in false stories and lies, and sometimes even fake personas and forced behavior. If you find yourself doing this, your attempt at socializing will backfire. Fake people attract other fake people, and this will repel meaningful connections.

## 5. Recognize that you have something to contribute

We've all lived unique lives and we need to recognize there's something about all of us that makes us interesting. No one has lived exactly the same life as you. You may share the same hometown, the same parents, or even a similar trauma to someone else, but no one possesses the same combination of upbringing, experiences, and choices as you. This means you're unique and you have something to contribute that no one has ever heard before. You need to recognize that you have valuable insights. You may feel shy or reserved, but consider the fact that other people in the conversation might benefit from hearing your point of view.

## 6. Understand that not everyone is as confident as they seem

You're not alone. Chances are high that even the person you're talking to is fighting their shier urges. While there certainly are many extroverted and socially comfortable people out there, the majority of people identify as an introvert. Even wildly successful individuals like Mark Zuckerberg and Steven Spielberg are known to have shy and anxious tendencies. Yet you'd never guess it with the number of public appearances they've both made and, most importantly, with how confident they come across. Know that you, too, can seem this confident, even if you don't feel that way deep down inside.

# Chapter 3 - Igniting Exceptional Interactions

You've made it past first impressions and you've pulled them into a full on conversation. Now what? At this point, many people find themselves at a loss for words, unsure of what exactly to say next. You've already asked them how they've been, what they did over the summer, and told them how great their outfit is. Now, they're looking at you expectantly and you have no idea how to fill the silence.

We all crave engaging discussions and a genuine bond, but when you're standing in that silence, it can feel impossible. How can we make what we say mean something? What can we do to break away from hum-drum hellos and how-do-you-dos? How can we be interesting conversationalists?

## Conversation Topics & Tips for Every Possible Scenario

Depending on the exact circumstances, certain topics may be more or less appropriate for the occasion. Nevertheless, there are a great deal of topics that can ignite fascinating discussion, regardless of context.

For the most successful delivery, it's advised to work in new topics as naturally as possible instead of simply blurting out a question. For best results, try and include an interesting story or observation that is relevant to the topic.

### Friends

We should feel comfortable around our friends, but there are many scenarios in which we might not. For example, with new friends. Or perhaps, if you're talking one-on-one with a friend that you normally see with a group. Dynamics also change depending on how many people are involved, and it's wise to adjust communication methods to the exact context.

# Job Interview Preparation

With groups, it's a good idea to ask questions that give everyone the opportunity to contribute and share. Asking overly personal questions in a group setting may make someone feel put on the spot, and it's likely the whole group doesn't want to slow down to listen to one person's story for a long time. Keep questions, in these scenarios, open to everyone.

When you're in a one-on-one talk, on the other hand, conversation can be highly engaging if you ask them questions you wouldn't normally ask. Take a look at these examples for some ideas:

<u>New Friends</u>

- How long have you known each other and how did you meet?
- What does everyone think about that latest episode in [insert TV show here]?
- What did everyone do last weekend?
- Does anyone have any funny bad date stories?
- What is everyone binging on Netflix right now?
- What's the craziest thing you've seen on the news recently?
- Has anyone here ever met a celebrity? If so, what happened?
- What's the most trouble you've ever gotten into?
- If your life story was turned into a movie and this moment made it into a scene, who would play you and who would you choose to play everyone else?
- How would you say you've changed since High School?

<u>One-on-One Conversations</u>

- How is work going?
- Are you seeing anyone these days?
- What do you think of [random mutual friend]'s new girlfriend/boyfriend?
- How often do you see your family?
- What's the most embarrassing thing that's ever happened to you?

- Do you consider yourself an introvert or an extrovert?
- How many relationships have you had and which one shaped you the most?
- What's the worst sexual experience you've ever had?
- What are some goals you're currently trying to achieve?
- Have you ever gotten into a physical fight?
- Which world cultures are you most fascinated by?

**Work Acquaintances**

There will be a range of intimacy levels with work acquaintances. Some you may be very comfortable with while others feel distant. Regardless of how well you get along, it's always best to keep conversations with colleagues somewhat professional. This doesn't mean that all talks need to be stiff and formal, it simply means they should remain within a narrow realm of topics. With the exception of rare circumstances, questions that are personal will not be seen as appropriate.

- If you didn't have this job, what would you be doing instead?
- What do you like to do on the weekends?
- How do you recharge after a long workday?
- Do you have any tricks for making it through a stressful workday?
- What's the weirdest job you've ever had?
- Have you ever had a crush on a coworker?
- If you could have lunch with anyone in the world, who would it be?

**Family**

Unlike our friends and romantic partners, we don't choose our family. And shared DNA doesn't always mean shared interests. It's not uncommon for family time to be awkward. Whether it's your family or someone else's family you're spending time with, one thing is for sure: family topics are always welcome. A great conversation starter is to ask about a specific family story, or question them about their earlier family life. This can spark a fascinating story and the chosen family member will feel touched by your curiosity.

Your Family

- Do we have any precious family heirlooms?
- What's our ancestry?
- What was your favorite pastime when you were a child?
- Do we have any interesting family secrets that I don't know about?
- Are we related to anyone famous?
- Who do you think I'm the most similar to in our family?
- What are some dominant familial traits?
- What's the most awkward moment you've ever seen at a family gathering?
- What was the first job you ever had?
- What are some of the biggest ways the world has changed since you were younger?
- What was [random family member] like when he/she was younger?
- How did [married family members] meet? (also feel free to ask this question directly to the subjects)

**Romantic**

There is a little more wiggle room when it comes to conversations with a romantic interest. This is because both parties are often actively trying to get to know each other, so questions that would normally seem out-of-the-blue are not that unusual. For example, if you're talking to a regular acquaintance and ask them, "How long was your longest relationship?" they may consider this question very personal and nosey. But on a date with a romantic interest, getting to know each other is expected. After all, you are trying to test how compatible you are.

- What are your guilty pleasures?
- Are you close with your family?
- Are you more like your mother or your father?
- What were you like as a teenager?
- How long was your longest relationship?
- How do you think you've changed in the last 10 years?
- What's your love language?
- Do you prefer fun nights out or cozy nights in?
- If you could settle down in any country in the world, which one would you choose?
- What's a movie, song, or book that has really shaped the way you see the world?
- What's your weirdest or most interesting habit?
- What's your favorite way to experience nature?
- What's your dream job?
- Who are your best friends and why?
- Do you consider yourself an introvert or an extrovert?
- What was the most challenging aspect of your childhood?
- How comfortable are you with public displays of affection?
- What would you consider a deal-breaker in a relationship or potential partner?

## The Worst Mistakes You Can Make in a Conversation

Once we begin actively talking to someone, there are many reasons the interaction could fall flat. It's not always for the reason you think and chances are, even though you think you're socially adept, you're making at least one of these mistakes.

1. **Talking about yourself too much**

If you come across as a narcissist, you can say goodbye to a genuine human connection. While people may enjoy learning about you, you shouldn't expect them to listen to long stories about your life without asking for theirs in return. It takes two to form a connection, and if there's no space for another person in the conversation, what's the point? If you notice yourself continuously changing the subject to you and your life, stop and ask your conversation partner something about their life. Listen carefully while they tell their story, and do not respond with something about yourself each time. Instead, try to acknowledge what they've said and extend understanding or an observation.

### 2. Acting like a know-it-all

Due to our need for expansion, we enjoy being around smart people. We don't, however, enjoy being around know-it-alls. You may be wondering what the difference is, and the answer is simple: know-it-alls are smart people who constantly feel the need to prove they're smart. Do you go on long tangents, explaining complex or obscure ideas to people who don't care and didn't ask for an explanation? Do you go out of your way to demonstrate your breadth of knowledge because you want recognition? You might be a know-it-all. This can be another form of narcissism but occasionally, it can signify a lack of-self esteem. Know-it-alls are sometimes so insecure that they latch onto the one trait they feel confident about, their intelligence. If this sounds like you, resist the urge to prove how smart you are all the time. This will only push people away. After all, if you're acting above them, how can they form a connection with you?

### 3. Being pedantic

Pedantry can sometimes signify a know-it-all, but not all the time. Even unintelligent people can be pedantic. What makes a pedant? Someone who is overly concerned with unimportant details and rules. They will go out of their way to correct people about trivial facts, even if it has no bearing on the conversation.

Let's say you're telling a new acquaintance about something amusing that happened to you and your friend, Rhonda, who is also present.

"We were just at a restaurant on 3rd and Geary Street," you begin to say, "And a woman asked for my autograph. Turns out she mistook me for a celebrity!"

You and your new acquaintance laugh, but Rhonda says, "Actually, the restaurant was on 3rd and Brady, not Geary." In this scenario, Rhonda is being pedantic. This detail is not important to the story, but she had to chime in anyway. After this comment, there is likely to be an awkward pause in the conversation. Don't interrupt the good mood for an insignificant detail. Avoid the urge to correct people if it makes no difference to the conversation. Let it go!

### 4. Oversharing

We all want to form an emotional connection. Intimate friendships or relationships can be great catalysts for this. When you share information that is too personal with someone you are not close to, however, this is called oversharing. Let's turn to socially awkward Rhonda again. She's meeting up with a new friend for the first time and they're having a casual lunch in town. She realizes that it's Monday the 3rd, and she suddenly remembers that her parents got divorced on Monday the 3rd many years ago. She begins telling her new friend all about the trauma she endured when her parents became divorced.

The new friend has just been on the receiving end of oversharing. Rhonda doesn't know her new friend that well yet, and she has already started sharing something extremely personal. This puts the other party in an uncomfortable place because they are still casually getting to know you, but now they feel they need to console you. Save your personal stories for after you know a person reasonably well.

### 5. Being pretentious

Pretentiousness is very common, and we're all guilty of it sometimes. We can be pretentious for many reasons. Perhaps, we want to look more cultured, more popular, or just generally more interesting. A know-it-all can also be classified as being pretentious if their intention is to impress someone. A pretentious person tends to enjoy showing off and exaggerating some aspect of themselves. They may want to impress people by demonstrating they've read obscure books that most people don't understand, or perhaps they are constantly name-dropping famous people they've met to seem more influential. Whatever it is they're trying to demonstrate, no one likes a pretentious person. This is because pretentious people are playing a game, and others can sense it. Since people respond more positively to honesty and sincerity, pretentiousness can ruin your chances at getting someone to like you.

### 6. Not paying attention

We've all met someone like this. Sometimes they are narcissists who can't stop talking about themselves, but other times they may just appear disinterested and distracted. However it manifests, we've all had a conversation with someone who doesn't seem to be listening to what we're saying. It seems as if they're only waiting for their chance to respond. Not listening to our conversation partner is a major social faux pas. The other person can always tell and even if they don't show it, it's probably annoying them.

### 7. Preaching and lecturing

We tend to associate this kind of behavior with our parents or teachers – if you don't want your new friends to think of you as a nagging and annoying presence, then stay away from all forms of preaching and lecturing. Judgmental people can be prone to this kind of behavior, but other times it can be the result of attempted helpfulness gone wrong. It occurs when one party feels they know the best course of action on a particular subject, and instead of talking to their peers about it as an equal, they end up talking *at* them. Someone who engages in this behavior will constantly try to tell people what they 'should' do, and ramble on in the same way a parent does.

If you disagree with something an acquaintance or friend did, try asking questions to incite reflection. Or perhaps share a similar experience that you've had or heard of, and explain what the consequences were. Do this in a gentle and compassionate manner. There are many ways to make a suggestion without preaching.

### 8. Being easy to offend

The modern day has opened up many important conversations about the way we treat each other. Some people, however, have taken this a little too far. They insist on being offended even by minor things and will go out of their way to shove blame on anyone. If it's clear that no harm was intended, chill out and let it go. If someone says something ignorant out of a lack of knowledge instead of nastiness, gently enlighten them and then move on. People who are easily offended or upset cause others to feel as though they are walking on eggshells. And guess what? No one wants to talk to a person that makes them feel this way.

### 9. Talking badly about other people

It's a cheap trick to try and bond with someone. You don't know what else to talk about, so you try to connect with someone over mutual dislike for others. Sometimes it can even be a backwards way of complimenting the person you're talking to. For example, "You have such a beautiful home! Have you been to Jessica's house? Her decor is *so* tacky. And Kate's house is a total mess. You definitely have the nicest home of all." Unfortunately, this does work on some people, but this behavior is commonly associated with teenagers and high school politics. Friends who take on this dynamic encourage the worst parts of each others' personalities.

If you're looking to create a healthy connection that truly enriches your life, we don't advise talking badly about other people. Mature, secure, and emotionally stable individuals will immediately be repulsed by such behavior. If you are willing to talk this way about other people you know, there's little stopping you from talking this way about them.

Job Interview Preparation

# Ideas to Steer Clear of Boring Conversations

Let's start off with a hard truth: some boring conversations cannot be prevented. Why? Because it takes more than one person to make it interesting. You can say all the right things and pull out the most effective techniques, but if the other person is obstinate and closed-off, then you can't control their behavior.

The good news is these instances are a rarity. Most shy and serious people can be pulled out of their shell with the right coaxing. Truth is, everyone has a humorous, interesting, or unusual side to them – you just have to find out how to access it.

### 1. Share an embarrassing or unusual story

Conversations become boring when no one is taking any risks. No one is sharing anything new, they're just saying what they feel they are supposed to say. When someone shares a genuine thought, feeling or observation, however, you'll notice your mind waking up. We are wired to find truth and honesty interesting, because it's something we can all connect with. It sends a signal that we can be ourselves. If you want to open up a new acquaintance and get them to expose a side of their personality they don't show anyone, you must create a safe environment for them. A great way to get the ball rolling is to share a story of your own. If it makes you seem a little vulnerable, they'll be far more engaged and likely to share something similar with you.

### 2. Identify passions and ask about them

It's a no-brainer: everyone loves to talk about what they're passionate about. Listen out for what people say they enjoy and ask them for more details once you learn what it is. This might be someone's job, but not always since a lot of people don't really enjoy their jobs. To find out what these passions could be, pay attention to what people said they did on the weekends or don't be shy, just ask them what their favorite hobbies are!

### 3. Ask an open-ended question

You are completely within power to redirect the course of a conversation if you so desire. A great way to do this is by asking questions. Stay away from 'yes' or 'no' questions, however, since this will give people the opportunity to give a short answer. An open-ended question will force them to elaborate and take their answer to a more interesting place. Since they'll have to think more about their answer, they'll be more engaged in the conversation. Instead of the question "Do you enjoy your new job?" try asking "What is it like at your new job and what do you enjoy about it?" If all else fails, ask for their honest opinion on something.

### 4. Respond genuinely and elaborately

We've already established that people respond to honesty. That's why you should always respond to people genuinely, and without any pretenses. Please note that this is different from being brutally honest, where we may share an inappropriate or hurtful truth. Being genuine simply means we are not trying to be someone we are not. When we speak elaborately, we give the other person more to respond to.

### 5. Embrace your silly side

In other words, tell a joke every now and then. Bring some humor into the way you speak. Just keep it appropriate and mature, avoiding all humor that degrades another person. Silliness does not just mean silly faces or pranks (avoid this unless you're with good friends!) it means infusing a sense of the ridiculous into your conversation.

### 6. Lighten up

We all want to avoid boring conversations, but listen, don't stress yourself out. Chances are your conversation partners can tell when you're trying extremely hard. It may even manifest in over-seriousness or too much intensity which can put people off. Part of the trick is to just take it easy and enjoy yourself. Lighten up. Keep all these tips in mind but be natural and exude positivity, no matter how the conversation is going.

## Three General Rules for Sparking an Interesting Conversation

### 1. Bring up something *you* find interesting

One way we tend to sabotage a conversation is by only bringing up the topics we feel we're supposed to bring up. We stick to safe topics because we think that's what's expected of us. Unfortunately, this is a pretty common formula for a boring conversation – and why would you expect anything more than that? After all, even you don't really care about these topics, do you? To truly make a conversation interesting, bring up a topic you're actually fascinated by. There's a good chance that if you find it engaging, the other person will too.

### 2. Deepen conversation topics over time

It's completely normal to start off with a lighthearted topic. We all need to ease in. However, we can always make our conversations more interesting by taking them to a deeper level. And don't be scared of the word 'deep.' It doesn't mean you need to talk about existentialism or traumatic heartbreak. It just means that you need to get to the core of the subject and make it completely relatable.

For example, let's say two people start off talking about their cats and all the funny, adorable habits their little feline friends have. If they just stick to this aspect of their cats, they'll eventually run out of things to say. To keep things interesting, they need to take the topic to new depths. They should tell the stories of how they found their cats, complete with the emotions of it all, and they should discuss how it is that their cats bring so much to their lives. They could ponder interesting questions about pet-owner relationships, or what unique benefits a cat brings and a dog doesn't. Deepening a topic creates a bond. Try it in your next conversation.

### 3. Be as specific as possible

Speaking in vague and general terms is a sure way to bore and frustrate your conversation partner. If someone asks you what you like to do on the weekends, don't just say, "I like to go out with friends." Give a more complete answer. When we offer up generalities, it doesn't give our conversation partners any material to respond to. This can result in awkwardness or strained conversation. It also sends the message that you're not very enthusiastic about the conversation at hand.

Instead of the above statement, say something more detailed like, "I like to go out with friends. We enjoy nightclub-hopping on the weekends and when that gets too much, we like to take road trips out into nature." The amended statement opens up two new doors: nightclubs and nature. Always aim to open new doors with your responses. Make it easy on your new acquaintances!

# Chapter 4 - Cultivating Charisma and Magnetism

It's one thing to have pleasurable conversations every now and then, but what if you want more than that? Some of us are blessed with charisma and magnetism. This means you don't have to pursue interesting interactions and people, instead they seem to find you. A small portion of people are gifted and naturally magnetic, but the rest of us shouldn't give up hope. Like most things in life, you don't have to be gifted to be good at something. You just need the self-awareness, knowledge, and the practice.

We've all met someone with charisma and magnetism. People are drawn to them like moths to light, purely because their presence is energizing and enjoyable. Magnetic individuals take communication skills to a new level entirely. They know which rules should be followed strictly, which ones should be broken, and which ones are exceptions in certain circumstances.

Magnetic individuals find it easier than most to achieve career success, large friend groups, and a wide variety of romantic options. The development of these qualities is no easy feat, but it can be done. First, however, you need to know the secrets.

## The Thirteen Secrets to Developing a Magnetic Personality

### 1. Cultivate emotional self-sufficiency

Arguably one of the most powerful qualities to develop, emotional self-sufficiency is a major driving force behind magnetic individuals. Quite simply, it signifies an ability to monitor your own emotions and needs, and understand exactly how to satisfy them without outside help. There is no dependence on other people to take care of their needs because they know how to do it themselves. They have mastered the teaching of 'You cannot control other people's actions, only your reactions' and they live closely by it. They focus on what they can control and nothing more. Other people are drawn to this quality because it makes a person seem stable, secure, and smart. We tend to trust someone who has control over their emotions as it gives the impression of maturity.

## 2. Your presence must give just as much as it takes

A truly magnetic personality does not operate from a 'me, me, me' philosophy. In fact, they make sure that other people in the conversation get something they need as well. Sometimes it's empathy, encouragement, gentle honesty, or even recognition. They are not afraid to compliment others, and when they do, it comes from a genuine place, instead of just wanting to score points. They might share interesting stories about themselves, but more than this, they are curious about other people, they ask questions, and they share comments that are both helpful and authentic. When people benefit from an interaction with you, whether it's mentally or emotionally, they are far more likely to seek your company again.

## 3. Learn to balance intelligence, humor and kindness

These three qualities are some of the most difficult to learn but when used in tandem, they can be irresistible. Intelligence allows us access to a large pool of data, humor makes it fun, and kindness creates the bond. People with strong magnetism utilize this trifecta to their advantage and with it, they charm people instantly.

## 4. Don't be afraid of vulnerability

Many people make the mistake of coming across too tough and impervious. Contrary to popular belief, this is not a good way to attract interesting connections. While it may temporarily impress or even intimidate people, it won't make anyone crave your company. This is because machismo or toughness is a pretense, and it will only attract people putting on the same pretense. Magnetic people are not afraid of being vulnerable. If it's relevant and appropriate, they have no issue sharing a heartfelt comment or allowing someone a glimpse into their true feelings. They do so in a manner that does not seek attention or overshare. People are drawn to this because we are engaged by sincerity.

### 5. Learn how to read people like a book

It takes more than one person to create a successful social interaction. This is why a great communicator doesn't just focus on their own behavior, they also notice how others behave. They are masters at reading and interpreting signals to determine the mood of anyone around them. This skill is important because a person's mood can change constantly, and it will shape the way they perceive the world. This means that a persuasion tactic that works on happy Person A might not work on anxious Person B. Using what they gather from observation, magnetic people are able to adjust their tactics and behavior so as to elicit any desired response from anyone.

### 6. Stop publicizing everything

Magnetic people value privacy greatly, and you may even find that some of them carry an air of mystery. Do not try to become intentionally mysterious, as this is likely to backfire. Instead, learn to hold certain memories and experiences as sacred. Learn to see the value in privacy and stop publicizing everything about your life. Share deeply personal matters with a select few and resist blabbermouth tendencies. Someone who shares personal details incessantly comes across as overly-emotional and as having no control. These are qualities that tend to repel people instead of attracting them.

### 7. Learn to adapt

This valuable skill can only be learned through experience and trial-and-error. Once gained however, it will get you far. Magnetic individuals can adapt to a range of different scenarios and can get along with many kinds of people. Men, women, young, old, and even people from other cultures. They can pick up on the rhythm and communication style of their conversation partner, the type of stories they value, and they can adjust their behavior accordingly. At the end of the day, they know that whoever it is, you can always connect to the aspects of humanity that we all have in common.

### 8. Make the best of what makes you different

While there are certain social codes that are absolutely necessary, magnetic individuals are not fussed about total conformity. As long as they're dressed well and appropriately, they see no reason why they should wear the exact same style as everyone else. As long as they're being polite and considerate, why should they stick to the same humdrum conversation topics that everyone else is discussing? Magnetic people won't go out of their way to stand out from a crowd, but they will embrace their natural eccentricities and proclivities.

### 9. Stop feeling embarrassed about every misstep

There are certain situations in which shame and embarrassment are deserved. For instance, if something mean we've said or something unethical we have done is exposed, then we should feel shame for those actions. But if no harm has been done or intended, a magnetic person rejects feelings of embarrassment. Why? Because, at the end of the day, only we can embarrass ourselves.

Perhaps, you showed up to a party and are wearing the exact same outfit as another person. Consider these two opposite ways of reacting to this scenario:

- You sink into the nearest armchair and hope no one notices you. You immediately start telling your friend, "I can't believe it! I need to leave or find a new outfit." As you talk, you and your friend continue to look at this person, and they notice. Your face turns red, and everything about your body language says you don't want to be seen. The other party attendees notice the similar clothes, and since you are noticeably embarrassed, they are embarrassed for you. It affects your interactions for the rest of the night, as people are turned off by your awkward behavior.

- You notice the person in the same clothes and can't help but see the amusement in the situation. What are the odds? You go up to the other person and say jokingly, "Can I just say you have a fantastic sense of style?" You both laugh, and so do the people around you. It is no longer an awkward situation because you have made light of it. The party attendees respect you for being able to laugh at yourself. Since everyone has seen what a great sense of humor you have, people want to converse and joke around with you for the rest of the night. After a while, no one even thinks about the similar clothes.

The moral of the story is: the only difference between people laughing *at* you and laughing *with* you, is that you're not laughing as well. If you choose to see the humor in your 'embarrassing' moments, you can never be humiliated.

See the absurdity in every situation and always continue to have a good time. Ask yourself, "What difference does this make in the grand scheme of my life?" The answer is likely, "No difference at all."

### 10. Realize there's something to learn from everyone

There's no such thing as truly boring people. Everyone is interesting if you get to know them, and everyone has something to contribute. Magnetic people recognize this. In a new crowd, they stay aware of everyone's unique and positive qualities and they learn from them, when possible. Pay attention to what makes your acquaintances different and use that to hone in what you could learn from them. It could be anything from an effective negotiation strategy or a comedic sensibility to unique stories about a faraway culture or a complex industry you know nothing about. Stay open to learning and allow others to teach you.

### 11. Don't be afraid to say you don't know

When we encounter a topic that we don't understand, many feel the need to pretend to know more than they do. This can suffice for quick encounters when there's not much time to chat, but at all other times, one should never feel ashamed of saying, "That's interesting, I never knew that."

Let's say, you're talking at length with someone and they start bringing up the economy, it's possible that this is a topic you don't know much about. Have the confidence to say, "This sounds fascinating. Tell me more about how it works." You can even use this opportunity to compliment and get to know someone. You could say, "I wish I knew more about this, but I never took time to learn. How did you become so knowledgeable?" We tend to trust people who are open about their shortcomings, as it makes them seem humble, self-aware and comfortable with who they are. It allows us to let our guard down. Furthermore, when we give someone the opportunity to feel like they can teach us something, it makes them feel significant and interesting.

## 12. Do not give any attention to someone who doesn't respect you

We've established that magnetic people are intelligent and empathic, but a necessary quality is also self-respect. You can be kind, complimentary, and try your best to get to know someone, but if they begin behaving rudely, you must drop that social interaction like a hot potato. If you allow someone to disrespect you, then other people will realize they can get away with this behavior. It sends a signal that you have no self-respect and will put up with abuse. Distance yourself from anyone that disrespects you and if you can't, then it's time to brush up on your classy comebacks.

## 13. Build a large network of diverse connections

It can be tempting to only connect or befriend people from your industry of work, but this isn't the way of a magnetic person. Include a diverse range of people in your social circle. Open yourself up to individuals from other cultures, genders, sexual orientations, religions, work industries, and more. Not only can it feel fulfilling to have a large group of friends, but you'll come across as multi-faceted and well-connected.

## All You Need to Know About the Trifecta of Charm

The trifecta of charm consists of intelligence, humor, and empathy. When combined in the right way, this formidable combination of qualities can charm almost anyone. In some cases, it can even override your physical appearance, making you come across as attractive even if you are not conventionally so. While most people embody at least one of these traits, they must work together to produce the best results.

In a conversation, intelligence alone makes one seem stiff and inaccessible, while someone gifted with only humor will come off too childish and silly. Empathy is a valuable trait, but without intelligence or humor it creates an individual that is too soft and overly emotional. The trifecta of charm utilizes all three at once and in equal measure.

Unfortunately, these qualities are also some of the most difficult to teach. In order to develop them, individuals must work hard at assimilating new habits into their personality, and must engage in a significant amount of study. Some trial-and-error may be necessary, and personal style will vary with each person. Still, it is absolutely possible for someone who scores low on all three counts to add the trifecta of charm to their social arsenal. They need only follow these tips:

- **Intelligence**

Intelligence can be described in a number of different ways, but at its core, it's comprised of several basic functions. Problem-solving, reasoning, logic, and critical thinking are some of the most notable. Many believe you're either intelligent or you're not, but this has proven to be far from the truth. Intelligence can always be developed, even in adults. It only requires that people challenge themselves, explore unfamiliar topics and try to assimilate them into their understanding of the world.

You may be wondering why intelligence matters in a conversation. Quite simply, it is easier for intelligent people to connect the dots and expand on any topic that is presented to them. They are sources of interesting information and people tend to like someone they can learn from, as long as the person isn't condescending or hijacking the conversation.

To enhance your intelligence, make sure to:

1. **Expand your mind in a way that you enjoy**

People tend to shy away from this suggestion because they think it means they need to read a heap of books. While reading can definitely expand your mind, there are a variety of other options to better suit your preferences. You can learn about new topics by watching documentaries, educational YouTube videos, television shows, enrolling in a class, taking an online course, or perhaps by asking someone who knows more than you on a certain topic. Information can be transferred in countless ways. You just need to discover what way works best for you.

2. **Discuss a topic with someone who has a different opinion from you**

Learning to have a civil discussion with someone you disagree with is a highly valuable skill. By challenging our perspectives, they force us to reason and think critically, and let's face it, debates can be exciting. Even if you feel strongly that the other person could not be more wrong, it's an excellent exercise for developing your sense of logic. And sometimes we don't realize there's a flaw in our reasoning until we are faced with a challenger. We can learn from their good points as well as their flawed arguments. All we advise is that you keep it civil! Remember, attack the arguments, and not the person making them.

3. **Practice explaining the new things you've learned**

It's no use reading lots of information if we can't actually retain it. One way to ensure you keep all that new data in your head is to try and explain it to someone else. This can be anyone – a partner, a friend, or if you're feeling confident, a new acquaintance.

- **Humor**

To truly enjoy someone's company, there must be some level of humor. It forces us to take it easy, keep it light-hearted, and to see the joy in even the most absurd situations. Without humor, the world would be a miserable place, and this is why it's a vital component of the trifecta. Making someone laugh is an easy way to start developing a connection. In fact, humor is so powerful, it can make people overlook a range of negative qualities.

It's also important to note that having a good sense of humor also requires you to be able to take a joke. If someone pokes fun at you and they don't intend to be mean, try to see the humor in it! Laugh it off and don't be easily offended. And remember, the best kind of humor is not mean or degrading towards another person. Keep it smart and inoffensive.

1. **Immerse yourself in comedic entertainment**

There's no better way to understand the workings of good comedy than by finding comedic entertainment that you enjoy. Watch a funny TV show, movie, stand-up performance, or even YouTube videos. Expose yourself to a variety of comedy styles and choose the one you most enjoy. Try to stay away from comedy that revolves around pranks and slapstick humor. While it's totally fine to enjoy these, one shouldn't expect to learn anything from them.

2. **Practice seeing the absurdity in everyday scenarios**

This skill can be valuable not just for conversation skills but for life in general. It will teach you how to laugh in the face of disasters, and instantly ignite more positivity even on bad days. Laughter is, after all, one of the best remedies for all troubles. Life is filled with absurdity and ridiculousness, you just have to recognize it. The next time you find yourself annoyed by something, try turning it on its head and seeing it as a comedic scenario.

### 3. Surround yourself with funny people

We all know someone with a killer sense of humor, someone who's a joy to be around, and makes us laugh at the drop of a hat. A great way to become funnier or develop a better sense of humor is to spend time with funny people. Listen and laugh at their jokes, try to respond in a similarly lighthearted fashion, and try to learn from the way their humorize certain situations. Notice what they joke about, how they joke about it, and what exactly makes it funny. If there are jokes that fall a little flat, examine why. The best part of this humor-building tactic? You'll enjoy it immensely and spend more time with a friend!

- **Empathy**

Quite simply, empathy is the ability to put yourself in someone else's shoes. It means you can pick up on their emotions, and feel what they're feeling. It's more than just sympathy, empathetic individuals can feel other people's experiences as if they endured them as well.

Most of us are reasonably capable of cognitive empathy, which is when we understand emotion on an intellectual level, but we can't actually relate to what someone is feeling. Sometimes, we may not even really care, but we know what we're supposed to say to be polite. We can recognize that someone is sad, and we know how to act sympathetic, but there's no part of us that feels this person's sadness. We can think about emotions rationally, but all the while, we remain somewhat detached.

Cognitive empathy can prove useful in the workplace and quick everyday conversations, but if you're interested in deep connections, it won't be enough. Thankfully, developing your emotional empathy will also enhance your cognitive empathy, so why not start there?

1. **Become aware of your own emotions and engage in self-love**

It's an uncomfortable truth, but a truth nonetheless; it all begins with you and the way you deal with your emotions. If you're constantly suppressing your feelings and you never deal with them in an honest, healthy way, then it's likely you're unable to relate to the feelings of others. You may find that a part of you resists emotional empathy because it opens a locked box of feelings that you haven't yet dealt with.

2. **Learn the life story of someone you disagree with**

It's easy to empathize with a homeless person or a victim of abuse, but this doesn't prove you're an empathic person – only that you're not a sociopath. To truly build empathy, challenge yourself by delving deeper into the life of someone you disagree with. Try to detach yourself from the opposing view or opinion they hold, and instead try to see them as a unique human being who has led a complex life, no different to you or anyone you're friends with. The goal is not to like them or change your opinion, but instead, to see beyond your perspective and feel someone's experience. It's possible to empathize with someone's problems or issues, and not agree with the choices they made.

This exercise is likely to be more meaningful if it involves someone you know, but if you're not ready for such an encounter, it's possible to use a public figure you don't know personally. This step can be completed in a variety of ways. You can watch the biopic of a historical or famous figure, or if it's someone you know, you can try to get to know them over digital messages or in person. Build the conversation gradually so you don't come across as nosey. Start by asking them about their background or family and lead to questions about their goals or influences. You'd be surprised how much you can relate to someone you don't even like!

3. **Take the time to imagine what being someone else is like**

We've all done this for at least a fleeting second, but rarely do we take the time to do it in depth. Try it. It's an exercise you can do absolutely anywhere, and in any physical position. Choose someone you know reasonably well. Imagine what it was like to have their childhood. Consider what it was like to see their parents every single day. Think of what childhood needs might not have been met. What are this person's insecurities? Imagine what it's like to wake up every morning with those insecurities, and how it plays out in everyday interactions. What kind of situations would bring up those insecurities? Imagine what hardships could have led to those insecurities.

Visualize the experiences this person might have had to result in who they are today. And more than this, consider the privileges you have that this person doesn't. Even if they are wealthier and more successful than you, chances are there are still privileges you have that they don't. Perhaps you have a happier family, perhaps you've never been as unlucky in love, or maybe you have more supportive friends. Imagine what it's like to no longer have those privileges and acknowledge how different your life would be without them.

## Three Steps to Becoming a More Interesting Person

Let's tackle a big question, shall we? Whether we admit it or not, we all want to become a more interesting person. But what does that really mean? Charisma is a major component, but that's not all there is to it. The trifecta of charm can also be considered a dominant influence over how interesting we are, but still, there's a little more to it than that. At the end of the day, being interesting comes with its own attitude – an attitude of openness and eclecticism.

Just think about all the experiences you've had with captivatingly interesting people. It's true that sometimes what's interesting can be subjective, but there are definitely some overarching traits. There tends to be the feeling that the other person is almost a treasure chest of stories and ideas. They have surprises up their sleeve. They know and have seen far more than you. They can't be caught or grasped, cause they are always one step ahead.

Let's use these experiences as a baseline, and figure out how we can emulate them.

1. **Do interesting things**

Doesn't that seem obvious? If you sit at home, watch TV, and stay in your comfortable bubble, you're not going to be very interesting to other people. We all use our experiences as a reference; if you haven't had many varied experiences, you're not going to have all that much to offer to conversations, unless it's with other people who also haven't seen that much. Accumulate fantastic, adventurous, and diverse experiences. Delve into the unknown and push the boundaries of your comfort zone. Do something you never thought you would do and expand your horizons. Collect interesting experiences and you'll become more interesting, in turn.

2. **Think outside of the box**

People are too focused on what they should be doing or saying that they miss the entire point of being interesting. Try thinking outside of the box or turning a situation on its head. This is different to behaving like a rebel or violating social codes; this just means responding in a way that is unusual. For example, if everyone is telling stories about how well-behaved their kid is, make things interesting by telling a story about the funniest thing your kid ever did, even if it was a little bit naughty. If all your friends are wearing modern bikinis, wear a classy high-waisted bikini styled from the 80s. If all your friends are discussing their biggest success at work, instead talk about the biggest failure that you learned the most from. Make situations more interesting by responding differently.

3. **Be open-minded**

No one likes a closed-minded person; the only ones who do are other closed-minded people who are closed-minded about the same things. Stop being so easily offended or shocked and replace those feelings with awe and curiosity. Not only will that make you more absorbent to interesting information, but it will also make you a more interesting conversationalist. The reason we like open-minded people is because they convey a sense of freedom. We actually don't experience closed-minded people as more moral, intelligent, or wise; they come across as caged by their own beliefs. Open-minded individuals can still have strong beliefs, but they are so comfortable and free that they can still listen to alternative opinions. We admire this sense of openness and freedom in others. Instinctively we feel that if a person embodies this attitude, they must have seen a lot and have a lot to share.

Developing all the qualities in this chapter will enhance your conversation skills tenfold. In reality, having better conversations begins with our frame of mind, our social abilities, and the experiences we've had. Work on developing all these skills, and you'll notice conversations coming alive in your presence.

# Chapter 5 - Knowing Your Audience

You may be likable and charming, but no conversation arsenal is complete without the ability to read a room. A conversationalist that can read a room is able to pick up the thoughts, feelings and general personality of every person they observe or engage with. As we mentioned earlier, this skill is paramount to good communication as we need to understand the factors that influence whether our social tactics will succeed or not. The strategies to win over a shy person will likely annoy someone who is very outgoing, and vice versa. Someone who is in a bad mood will not be as receptive to certain social cues as someone who is in a great mood.

## Microexpressions

We think that facial expressions tell us everything but that's not the whole truth. A smile doesn't always indicate happiness, and a serious expression doesn't necessarily indicate nervousness or displeasure. If you want to know how someone is truly feeling, pay attention to their microexpressions.

Microexpressions are nonverbal signals that last anywhere from a fraction of a second to a few seconds – but rarely longer than that. They may be recurring, but if they are permanent, then it's likely the person in question is not trying to hide their feelings at all. Microexpressions occur when we momentarily let our guard down and display our true reaction. Most people have been taught to act polite and always keep a tight rein on their true feelings, and this is why microexpressions are so fleeting. As soon as we feel ourselves slipping, we immediately return to the face we put on for the world.

The emotions we hide are not always negative. We may try to hide our euphoria while we're on a date with a person we really like, or we may try to hide our excitement if we're holding back good news before an official announcement.

# Job Interview Preparation

Let's consider Rhonda again. While attending a friend's party, she meets a variety of different people with whom she interacts. Since she's not the most socially skilled person, she is met with a range of different reactions.

1. **Stress and impatience**

When Rhonda arrives at the party, she immediately comes across somebody she knows. She stops to talk to her old friend, and unbeknownst to her, she has stopped by a doorway, blocking someone from entering. The stranger stands behind her, clearing his throat, but Rhonda doesn't notice. He purses his lips and his nostrils flare for a moment. When Rhonda eventually takes notice, his jaw tightens before he regains his composure and walks to his intended destination.

2. **Frustration or anger**

While at the party, Rhonda runs into her ex. The relationship ended badly and mostly due to Rhonda's bad behavior. She doesn't recognize him immediately since he cut his hair and started wearing contact lenses. Sitting at a table with some acquaintances, she doesn't realize he is present as well, so she ignores him. The ex is fuming, still bitter about the way she treated him and even more now since she can't recognize him. While he fumes, he presses his lips together and continues to purse them intermittently.

3. **Disdain or dislike**

Rhonda notices two women having a conversation and she joins in. Unfortunately, she changes the topic and begins talking about herself quite incessantly. While Rhonda talks, one woman looks at her askance, only making eye contact with the corner of her eye. She keeps her head tilted away from Rhonda, a sign that she is not enthusiastic about this newcomer's presence and may even feel superior to her. She resists the urge to roll her eyes and in doing so her eyelids flutter with more blinks than usual, sending the message, "The nerve of this woman!"

### 4. Disagreement and contempt

Later on, Rhonda converses with a teacher and makes the argument, "Schools are killing the creativity of children." The teacher disagrees strongly with this, though he still tries to act polite. For a moment, he furrows his brows and asks, "How so?" When furrowed brows accompany narrowed eyes, it indicates disagreement or skepticism, but if the eyes are wide, this signals curiosity. As Rhonda continues, the teacher begins to feel a little contemptuous. One side of his mouth curls up very briefly while the other side remains still. Many people misinterpret this expression as a 'half-smile,' but this is incorrect. This is a classic sign of contempt, especially if the mouth is tight.

### 5. Fear

Someone who had a bad experience with Rhonda at a different party sees her approaching. As she notices Rhonda, her eyes widen for a brief moment, conveying a sense of vigilance. Fear is most easily identified by looking at the eyes. The mouth also reacts by widening horizontally. This is different from a smile where the corners are upturned, when fear is introduced, the corners pull back horizontally towards the ears.

### 6. Excitement or happiness

Even though Rhonda had negative impressions on a lot of people, the person who invited her to the party is happy to see her. Rhonda's friend is in the middle of a serious discussion with someone else, so she's trying to not look too happy, but when she notices Rhonda, her eyes look a bit brighter. Even though she's not smiling, both corners of her mouth turn up very slightly.

## The Six Types of Communicators & How to Win Them Over

Social psychologists have discovered there are six major communication styles. While each of us is more likely to communicate in one of these styles naturally, we can actually learn how to use the talents and traits of all the other styles. For the most part, each type of communicator responds best to those who communicate in the same way, but not all the time. See if you can determine which type you are. And most importantly, figure out how you would approach the other different styles.

- **Noble**

*Straightforward, focused, tells it like it is*

These communicators tend to make great leaders as they have no qualms about saying what needs to be said and participating in the difficult conversations. They are practical, direct, and many people respond well to them since they are always honest. They are not concerned with the feelings of others, preferring to be upfront and straightforward. This doesn't mean they are unfeeling people, they simply don't factor in emotions when they are speaking. Though they usually don't have bad intentions, sensitive people can become upset at what they say since it's often not worded in a considerate manner. They are uncomplicated and usually quite predictable.

To win a Noble communicator over, you must be clear, direct, and confident. Avoid overly flowery language as they don't see the point and will see it as frivolous fluff. Focus on the 'what' and 'how,' since Nobles are most concerned with the practical details than anything else. Give them all the information upfront as they won't chase you for extra details. Other than these general rules, you'll find you can say almost anything to a Noble since they are only concerned with truth and reality.

- **Socratic**

*Expressive, persuasive, intellectual, detailed*

Unlike Noble communicators, Socratic individuals enjoy the long, drawn out discussions with lots of details. These communicators tend to clash with Nobles since their methods of communication are almost completely opposite. It is rare that a Socratic communicator gets into a short chat; as soon as they open their mouth, it's easy for them to get lost in a tangent or a long, flowery anecdote. When they tell stories they add a lot of background information, preferring to present the whole picture. At times, they can seem to be lecturing.

To befriend a Socratic, listen to their long-winded stories with your full attention, and better yet, ask them questions. They enjoy interesting and unique individuals, so make sure to tickle their intellect. Bring up unusual but fascinating topics, and join them as they delve deeply into them with their hundreds of questions and insightful analyses. They prefer to deal with ideas, instead of feelings, though they are more receptive to emotions than Nobles.

- **Reflective**

*Patient, understanding, sensitive, wants to bond*

If you're a reflective communicator, there are likely a lot of people in your life who run to you with their problems. For better or for worse, people enjoy seeking out support from reflectives since they are known for being understanding and having great listening skills. Reflectives like to connect on an emotional basis and usually aren't that interested in sharing strong opinions. It doesn't come naturally to a reflective communicator to be assertive or direct, so they can be dishonest or even deceptive. They would prefer to not see anyone's feelings hurt, so they say what needs to be said to keep conversation harmonious. Reflectives are the most likely communicators to get interrupted or overlooked in conversation, since they usually don't express themselves in a strong or confident manner.

To win a Reflective over, open up a little and show some vulnerability. Find common ground with them and share your mutual passions or interests. To really capture a Reflective's attention, ask them questions and encourage them to open up to you as well. They are so used to listening to other people and letting someone else take the spotlight that they can feel overlooked. Give them some kind attention and you'll win them over, for sure.

- **Candidate**

*Pleasant, talkative, analytical, wants to be liked*

When we combine the Socratic and Reflective styles, we get the Candidate communicator. Candidates are warm, chatty, and usually have a pleasant air about them. They enjoy connecting with others by telling stories, and will always make the effort to keep conversation harmonious. When a problem arises, they believe that talking is the best solution, and they do so in an emotionally engaged manner. They are more truthful than someone with only a Reflective style, but they still try their best to avoid messy conflict.

To get on their good side, turn on your good listening skills and be patient while they talk. If you stop paying attention or end a conversation abruptly, the Candidate will likely feel very annoyed. Since they also have Reflective attributes, they are a lot more receptive to other points of view than a Socratic communicator alone. Win them over by really engaging with them, sharing genuine parts of yourself, and listening closely to their long, sometimes emotional, stories.

- **Magistrate**

*Intense, argumentative, persuasive*

The Noble and Socratic styles fuse together to create the big presence of the Magistrate. These individuals can be incredibly eloquent and persuasive, but while they excel as public speakers, they can be a little slow in their interpersonal relationships. It takes them longer to grasp individual needs and sensitivities, so they can sometimes act out of line and offend people closest to them. When we witness a Magistrate communicator speaking, it can seem like they'd make a phenomenal leader. Oftentimes, it can come across like a monologue or a grand speech. Unfortunately, Magistrates tend to divide audiences and at their worst, can be preachy and overbearing. You either love them or you hate them. In their personal lives, they can be argumentative, and they may even get into trouble at work.

To get close to a Magistrate, be unafraid of serious, deep discussions. They don't shy away from the dark topics that, they feel, convey the real truth of life. It's also necessary that you understand how to speak calmly and rationally in heated discussions without flying off the handle. Otherwise you may find yourself in a full-blown argument with a Magistrate. Also make sure to listen closely to the Magistrate as they feel strongly that what they're saying needs to be heard. To flatter them, make them feel like the revolutionary they think they are.

- **Senator**

*Strategic, adaptable, observant, versatile*

The most complex of the six, the Senator is often considered the most clever communication style. In conversation, the way they speak and the things they say are all carefully calculated to produce the outcome they desire. They have the unique ability to combine the skills of the other five styles to create a predetermined effect. They may speak like a Noble, but also have the listening skills of a Reflective. They are highly unpredictable, and many people who try to get to know them may perceive them as fickle.

Trying to coax a Senator into your corner is no easy task. Of the six communicators, they are definitely the most difficult to catch. This is because they are always changing, and often their behavior is determined by what they hope to achieve. This is not always a selfish pursuit, sometimes the goal can be to help other people get along. The exact goal depends on the individual personality. We advise observing Senators closely and paying attention to the transitions between communication styles. One can often identify what their goal is by noticing what method of communication they are using at that moment. Reflect whichever style they appear to be using.

# Conversation Tips for Special Audiences

As we've demonstrated, conversation tactics are not the same for everyone. And even though we've covered a wide range of personality types already, there are a few others we still haven't accounted for.

## Children

It shouldn't be so scary to talk to tiny humans, but many people don't have experience with children. If you have to meet a new partner's kid or bond with a younger cousin, it will not serve you well to be filled with anxiety – though it wouldn't be completely unfounded. After all, children can't talk about the same topics as adults. And what if you accidentally say something that scares them?

The reality is, it's not as difficult as you think, and children are a lot smarter than people give them credit for. Children tend to respond positively when adults lower themselves to their height. When you're not a looming giant, you're more approachable. When you speak, make sure to use positive language. Instead of just saying, "Your mom has told me a lot about you" try sweetening it up by saying "Your mom has told me so much about how talented and smart you are!" Remember that kids love the idea of adventure, so if you're going to tell them any stories, make sure it has a hint of adventure. And ask them questions about what they enjoy. Kids will warm up to you when they can talk about whatever excites them.

When you talk to a kid, fully embrace silliness and you'll definitely get on their good side. And remember, do not ever correct a child when they are speaking playfully! If they said they visited the land of unicorns, do not say "Unicorns don't exist." Instead, ask them what it's like there and if they made any unicorn friends.

## The Elderly

It's no secret that as people get older, they become less physically and mentally capable of behaving as they used to. One common mistake people make, however, is talking to them like they're children. While they may be a little slower, you'll find that most elderly individuals are still incredibly sharp, especially when you ask them about the passions of their life. Shoot them a few questions about how they met their life partner, the career they had, or where they came from, and you'll find that they suddenly regain all their wits (provided none of these questions trigger something traumatic!) and enjoy sharing the fascinating stories they hold. Bear with them if their memory slows down, and allow them to find their thoughts.

Always speak to the elderly like the adults they are. Dumbing down your speech is not only rude, but it can actually do harm to their mental processes. Why? For the same reason you'd suffer if someone dumbed down their speech towards *you*. It lowers their self-esteem and quickens the decline of their cognitive abilities because no one is allowing them to use their mind properly.

There are as many communication styles as there are human beings in the world. No two people communicate in the exact same way – but this guide will help you navigate the major personalities. To identify what their exact style is like, consider their age, background, culture, interests, and their general nature. Everything is a clue; pay attention.

# Chapter 6 - Building Deep Connections

At the end of the day, we all crave something beyond lighthearted banter or party discussions. We want to bond with others. We want to see our humanity mirrored in another person, and we want to mirror theirs. Many will even argue that this is what life is all about – learning to live in harmony with others so we can help each other excel. Whatever you believe, it stands true for everyone: we all need deep connections. Without them, we can even become more susceptible to mental illness.

Since we all need it to thrive, you'd think it would be easy to make lasting and deep connections. But for the majority of us, they are few and far between. Often the most meaningful connections we have are with people we've known for a long time.

There are many reasons we may find this feat difficult. Sometimes it's because we're afraid of intimacy. Sometimes it's because we can be judgmental, and we want to believe there's nothing we could possibly have in common with the people around us. And of course many times, we just don't have the necessary social skills. We want a meaningful connection, but we just don't know how to get from A to B.

Here's some good news: it's actually not as difficult as you think.

## Conversation Tricks to Instantly Build Rapport with Someone

### 1. Try to reflect their speaking style

Pay attention to the rhythm, length, and word choices with which someone speaks. To build rapport, try and mirror their style of speech. If there are words they use often, work them into your side of the dialogue as well. It's important, when doing this, to not copy them entirely, or they'll feel like you're making fun of them. To avoid this, a good rule of thumb is to never mimic someone's accent.

## 2. Seek out their advice

Instead of asking for someone's opinion, ask for their advice. Doing this will strengthen your bond. Why? For starters, you come across as being genuine (only honest people can admit they need advice!) and second of all, you're showing them you think they're a credible source of feedback. After this interaction, they are also likely to feel invested in the issue they advised you on and they may want to keep up with what happens. Just make sure you pay close attention to them and listen to what they're saying carefully.

## 3. Combine ideas

You don't have to be at a work meetup to brainstorm; you can do this with anyone. All it involves is playing off their ideas and expanding on them. When you brainstorm with someone, whether casually or seriously, you show them you've been paying close attention to them and that you take their ideas seriously. In addition to this, you may satisfy their need for expansion, by showing that you have something to offer them intellectually.

## 4. Paraphrasing

When we paraphrase what someone says, we repeat what they said in our own words. The paraphrase should always be combined with another statement such as "I understand." Or, it can be turned into a question with the addition of something to the effect of "Is that right?" Paraphrasing shows that you've listened, understood, and empathized with what they've said. For example, if your friend says, "I'm an insomniac so please excuse me if I seem a little out of it," you could say, "I understand. You didn't get enough sleep, so of course you feel exhausted and disoriented." By saying this, you're not adding any new information, only rephrasing the previous statement slightly.

## 5. Ask questions that involve 'how' and 'why'

If you're not sure what kind of questions to ask, think of something that begins with 'how' or 'why.' These types of questions create bonds because you're asking your conversation partner to search themselves for more elaborate and meaningful answers. For example, if your friend is talking about a high-pressure meeting she just finished. You could ask "How do you feel about it now?" or "Why do you think it went so well?"

Building rapport is essential to creating a bond with empathy and connection, but we won't get there immediately. It involves a lot more than conversation tactics.

## How to Form Meaningful Relationships

### 1. Let people in

All the other points on this list mean nothing if you don't let people in. Don't act cold and aloof as this forms a barrier between yourself and others. Instead, try to exude an inviting aura and allow them to get to know you, as much as you get to know them. People often make the mistake of feeling like a victim when other people don't take an interest in getting to know them. Do not fall into this victim complex. Instead, ask yourself: am I showing this person that I can be trusted? Am I allowing people to get close to me? Am I showing them what makes me a good friend?

### 2. Balance giving and taking

If your friend bought you lunch at your last hang-out, buy them a drink or meal at your next hang-out. Return generosity with generosity. If you aren't in a good place financially, offer to do something else for them. There is beauty in having a friend or family member that would do anything for us, but our responsibility as a good person is to never ask them to do *everything* for us. If you come to the realization that you've been talking about your problems non-stop for the last hour, take the time to ask your close connection how they are, and make sure to offer them the same patience. Always be aware of when you might be asking for too much. And if you must, then ensure you make it up to them.

It's also important to note that the reverse should also be avoided. If your friend continuously asks you for a lot, be honest about how you feel and create some boundaries.

### 3. Make time to maintain the bond

Once we form a bond with a new friend or partner, we need to make the effort to nurture this relationship. It doesn't matter how well we get along with someone else – if we never make time for them in our lives, this bond will slowly dissipate. And when a reconnection is made in the distant future, it'll feel like you're starting all over again.

The act of making time is a powerful one, and it sends an important message: I care enough about you to always find time for you. If one party embarks on a long travel experience, or moves to a different city, make the effort to do a weekly or fortnightly catch-up session on the phone. Avoid having a dynamic where you only speak when one person needs a shoulder to cry on. Even partners that live together must find time in their busy schedules to maintain the bond. Creating quality time is a necessary part of keeping a connection alive.

### 4. Eradicate all competitive behavior

When we're close to someone, it's easy to start comparing ourselves to them. If your friend or partner is further along in their career than you are, never allow feelings of envy to drive your actions. It's perfectly normal for a jealous thought to cross your brain, but never let it trigger a decision that affects them. It's totally fine to think, "Gee, Adam is really having an affect on all the girls at this party. I wish I could do that." But it is not okay to start telling someone about his most embarrassing moment just to take him down a peg. Recognize that you both have different strengths and weaknesses, and that life is not a competition. Look for inspiration in your relationships, not competition.

### 5. Know the purpose your relationship serves

Each person in our life helps us in a slightly different way. Recognizing the greater purpose they serve can ignite feelings of appreciation and will ultimately help us strengthen the bond. The gifts they bring to our lives are far more specific than just giving us emotional support or preventing us from feeling bored. If you think about it, each person we know provides us with a unique lesson. See if you can identify the people who continuously teach you these lessons – and work out which ones you teach other people.

- Embrace everything that makes you different.
- It's okay to cry and talk about your feelings.
- Opposites attract and help each other grow.
- Everything can be fun if you let it be.
- The world is full of amazing experiences and you need to chase them all.
- We must always face ourselves exactly as we are and strive to be better.
- Just enjoy things as they are, there's no need to make it complicated.
- A true friend is with you during your darkest hours.

## The Habits of Emotionally Intelligent People

Remember when we discussed how magnetic individuals are adept at emotional self-sufficiency? That's a major attribute of emotional intelligence. An emotionally intelligent individual can not only sense, understand, and empathize with the feelings of others, they also have a firm grasp on their own emotions.

Believe it or not, emotional intelligence is a bigger indicator of one's success than their IQ. While an IQ is more likely to earn you a particular job, your level of emotional intelligence will determine whether you keep that job, or whether you get promoted. More than this, however, emotional intelligence is vital for fulfilling personal relationships, whether it's with family, friends, or romantic partners. Some people are born with an intrinsic gift for emotional intelligence, but it's completely possible for others to learn and develop the skill over time. Let's examine the life-altering habits of emotionally intelligent people.

- **They always find common ground**

When in conversation with someone, emotionally intelligent people focus on the similarities instead of the potential conflicts. It doesn't matter who it is or how different that person seems to be, they always converse with the intention of finding common interests and values. Even if the person they're talking to openly disagrees with them about something, individuals with a high EQ choose to focus on the similarities. When faced with conflict, they have the maturity to say, "Let's agree to disagree."

- **They are self-aware**

Self-awareness is a key attribute of emotional intelligence. This means that an individual has a good understanding of who they are, how they feel, what their triggers are, and how they are most likely to react in a given scenario.

Let's take Sally, for instance. She's has an extremely high EQ. After a bad day at work, she recognizes that she's feeling anxious and sad. Her friends invite her to have dinner at the mall. She knows that when she's sad, she is more likely to shop and overspend, so she has the self-awareness to realize that being near a shopping mall is not a good idea.

- **They are masters of self-discipline and self-management**

Remember when Sally recognized that going to the mall on a bad day would have a terrible outcome? Awareness is one thing, but having the discipline to say no is another. Self-awareness and self-discipline go together like bread and butter. After all, what's the point of being aware of the best course of action if you can't bring yourself to actually take that action?

Emotionally intelligent people are not slaves to their impulses. They are not prone to big bursts of anger or indignation; they deal with their feelings privately and if something must be done, they go about it maturely. They have the strength of mind to suppress behavior that will only cause damage and destruction, even if it causes momentary agitation. They don't expect other people to take care of their feelings, instead they take care of themselves.

- **They are always aware of subtext**

Everyone knows there's a big difference between the words people speak and what they're *actually* saying. High EQ individuals are always aware of this subtext. They are masters at interpreting tones of voice, word pacing, and the general vibe given off by each person they meet. With everything that they gage through observation, they are able to understand what's not being said. Intuition and 'gut feelings' can also help with deciphering subtext. If you get a strong feeling about something, chances are you're onto some subtext.

- **They steer clear from blame games**

Emotionally intelligent people are masters of accountability and acceptance. When something goes wrong, they resist the urge to point the finger elsewhere. They recognize that it usually takes more than one person to create a certain situation. If we find out a friend talked about us behind our back, it's easy to put all the blame on them and say they shouldn't have been doing that. But what if your friend was saying she's angry because you owe her a lot of money and she doesn't think you'll ever pay her back? It's important that we recognize our part in every situation. It's not about feeling guilty, it's about admitting that we have more power than we realize and owning up to the repercussions.

It's true that sometimes we can fault one person for something that goes wrong. If you took all safety precautions and someone robbed you anyway, it seems very clear who should be blamed. Not you, but them. Avoiding the blame game doesn't mean you can never say that someone else made a mistake; it means that you don't get stuck in a loop of blame where you cause yourself to suffer more than you need to. It's the difference between thinking "That man made a mistake" and "What an awful man. How dare he? Now everything is ruined and it's all because of him."

## Why Self-Compassion is Important for Healthy Relationships

A well-known misconception about fulfilling relationships is the idea that we need to give, give, and give to our closest companions. Kindness and empathy towards others are important parts of every relationship, that's true, but it's imperative that we never neglect our own needs. In fact, a good rule of thumb is to treat yourself the way you would treat a good friend. We would never ask a friend to give until she has nothing, and so we should never ask that of ourselves.

Self-compassion helps us recharge so we can continue to do our best for the world we live in. When we drain ourselves of energy, we are more prone to depression, moodiness, or general exhaustion. We drain ourselves of everything we need to continue being a good friend. Indirectly, self-compassion helps the people we care about as well.

Here are the ways in which we can show ourselves self-compassion in our everyday relationships:

- Your friends want you to stay out late for a big night out, but you're exhausted from work and don't really want to go. Instead of forcing yourself to go out because everyone wants you to, put self-care first. Tell your friends: "I'm going to take a raincheck and stay home to rest. I'm extremely tired, so I know you understand. Let's do something else soon!"
- You're with a group of people who are all sharing raunchy sex stories. You've always been a more private person and you start to feel uncomfortable with the topic. When everyone looks at you expectantly, waiting for a story, don't feel

pressured. Just say: "I'd prefer to keep this part of my life private, so I'm going to pass." Or if you're with a closer group of friends, feel free to tell them, "I'm not really comfortable sharing such intimate stories. Could we change the topic?"
- You run into a friend that you aren't very close to. She hears you broke up with your partner and is pressuring to tell you everything that happened, even though you don't want to talk about it. Be kind to yourself, and don't give in to pressure if it causes you distress. Tell her: "I'm not ready to talk about it yet. It's still hard to think about, so I'll have to tell you another time. Thanks for your concern."
- If a family member said something extremely hurtful and they suddenly want to see you, be compassionate towards yourself and ask yourself if you're ready or if you even want to. When someone hurts us it can take a while before we feel safe around them again. This is not our fault, and we should always make sure we are ready for future interactions.

Healthy and deep relationships require both parties to be taken care of. To develop more fulfilling connections, make sure both sides get what they need every time – and yes, that means you too! Make sure boundaries are respected and balance is always attained.

# Chapter 7 - Difficult Situations & Social Blunders

It's bound to happen at some point. Unfortunately, it's usually when you least expect it. You think everything is going swimmingly and feel like you're as smooth as honey, but then the unexpected happens. Perhaps you say something you shouldn't have – an easy flub or a major no-no – or perhaps the circumstances are out of your control, and a real jerk comes out of nowhere, derailing all your well-played moves and making you look like a fool.

We're not perfect and neither is anyone else. Awkward moments *will* happen and some of them will be mind-numbingly cringeworthy. In addition to this, rude people are aplenty, and we're going to encounter them whether we like it or not. To become a master of conversation, it's necessary that you understand how to diffuse a difficult social situation. There may be rocky roads ahead, so it's best to gear up.

## How to talk your way out of difficult or awkward situations

Don't just sit back and go red in the face. There are many ways we can use speech and conversation to mitigate a difficult conversation. You'd be surprised by how much we can accomplish with these quick tips.

- **You offended someone**

There are many reasons you could find yourself in this difficult position. You might have encountered someone who was easy to offend, or maybe, just maybe, you said something legitimately terrible. The first step is always to apologize, whether you mean it or not, and let them know you didn't mean to offend them. The second step is up to you.

**i)** Insist you chose your words wrongly and that it wasn't what you meant to say. If you can, amend what you said with better, less offensive phrasing. You can also chalk it down to a lack of sleep or fatigue, and tell them you're not as articulate as you normally are.

**ii)** Take the fall, be vulnerable and shift power from you to the other party. For example, let's say you accidentally insulted the way your friend dressed for a party and she is noticeably upset. Clear things up immediately by saying, "I'm sorry. Actually it's me, not you. I'm feeling very self-conscious in this outfit, and you look great. I'm a little jealous, so I projected how I feel about myself onto you."

- **Someone openly insults you**

Awful, shocking, humiliating; these are some of the words you could use to describe the moment when someone insults you. It may be direct and outright, or heavily implied. Either way, it will likely shake you to your core.

The first step is to consider whether we were truly insulted. Oftentimes, we can perceive brutally honest statements as insulting, but really they are just based on a harsh truth we don't want to accept. If we find the insult is more factual than not, then accept what's being said, apologize if necessary, and adjust your behavior, taking into account this new feedback.

You may also figure out the insult was real, and that a person really did just attack your character. In that case, you may follow any of these steps:

**i)** Use humor to undermine and ridicule the insult. This one takes some skill but when done correctly, you can win over an entire audience.

**ii)** Stand up for yourself in an honest and calm way. This does not mean fighting back. If someone calls you an idiot for not knowing something, you can respond by saying, "I'm not an idiot. No one knows everything and we're all learning here." By defending yourself in a mature manner, you'll bound to come out of the situation on-top.

**iii)** Let it slide but bring it up in private, afterwards. If you're not quick on your feet, it's okay to say nothing or laugh it off for the time being. Later on, you can take the person aside and confront them about what they said. This option is more likely to get a meaningful reaction from the person who insulted you. After the heat of the moment, people often regret their mistakes. Be honest about how uncalled for and hurtful it was to be insulted. This direct confrontation may make this person apologize.

- **Someone tries to argue with you**

When we get into a conversation, most people make the effort to keep it harmonious. For many reasons, however, you may encounter someone with an argumentative approach. This can be because they feel passionately against something you said, or it may be down to their personality. Assuming you have no interest in entering this argument, you can follow any of these steps:

**i)** Say "Let's agree to disagree." Completely disengage from the heated discussion. Cut it off before it gets worse.

**ii)** Listen to the other person's point of view. At the end of the day, the person just wants you to see their side. Allow them to fill you in, all the while saying that you see their point. Acknowledge that they have interesting points, but avoid mentioning your opinion. Turning on your listening skills is another effective way to avoid an argument.

- **Someone hits on you obnoxiously and can't take a hint**

Women experience this more often than men. You could be anywhere, on a bus or at a party, and someone may decide to make a move. Through body language and the nature of your speech, you get across that you're not interested, but the flirty individual does not budge.

**i)** Tell them to stop. Sometimes it can feel like this is the worst thing you can do, but it's usually the most effective method. The other person can't take a hint so sometimes there is no other way but to tell them outright. It doesn't have to be rude if you're trying to let this person off gently. You could say, "You're making me feel uncomfortable. I'm really not interested. I have been trying to let you know discreetly, but perhaps I'm not being clear enough."

**ii)** Mention that you have a partner. In conversation, let slip that you have a boyfriend or girlfriend, or a husband or wife. If you can gush about them, the more likely they'll leave you alone. You can even do this if you don't have a partner; just be prepared to answer questions, if they ask.

**iii)** Seek out the company of a third person. If you're at a social gathering, ask someone else to join you or excuse yourself to join a different conversation. Don't be afraid to quietly tell another person (ideally of the same gender as you) that you need some help getting rid of an obnoxious flirt. Most people will sympathize with you and try to help.

- **You need to break up with a boyfriend or fire an employee**

These are some of the most difficult conversations to start. And yet, mastering how to do it can make a genuine difference in the rejected person's life. A bad rejection or relationship end can either lower someone's self-esteem, or empower them to grow. To ensure it's the latter instead of the former. Follow these tips.

**i)** Make the time and do it in person. Even though the situation is extremely uncomfortable for you, no doubt, don't rush through the talk and make the meeting as personal as possible. It's harder for the other person than it is for you, so make sure to allow them all the closure they need. If they don't get closure, there's a higher chance they'll take it badly and find it difficult to move on.

**ii)** Tell them the issues honestly, but also mention their potential. We should always be fairly honest about what's not working out. If you're breaking up with your partner because you feel like you're not compatible, it's okay to tell them that. But make sure to also mention something that will not make them feel like a failure. Empower them to find another partner or employer. If you're parting with them because of an existing problem, give them constructive advice for how to grow. Also be prepared for the possibility they will give you feedback as well.

**iii)** End the conversation on a positive note. It may be a sad and awkward occasion, but there's no reason it has to end on that note. Wish them good luck in all their future endeavours. Tell them you're so sure they'll find a job or partner that's right for them, very soon!

## Coping with Difficult Personalities

It doesn't matter how many social tactics you have up your sleeve; when a difficult person comes into play, sometimes they can be intent on ruining the mood or heating up a conversation. For a number of difficult people, it is just the way they are, but it's important to note that for the majority of people, it could just be a bad day or a rough period in their life. While this doesn't excuse their behavior, it should encourage us to empathize with them and resist the urge to be nasty.

Before we discuss the specific types of difficult personalities, here are three general rules to keep in mind:

- Consider what their real need is. What is it they really want that they don't know how to get in a healthy way? There can be general needs that are common to certain personality types, but often they can be specific to the individual.

- Stay calm and listen to what they're saying before you respond.

- Take the high road and continue to treat them with respect.


**1. The Egomaniac**

Egomaniacs have an inflated sense of self-importance and somehow conversation always seems to lead back to how great they are. They can be overt egomaniacs, talking shamelessly about their accomplishments, but sometimes it can be subtle. Many attempt to seem like a normal person, but you'll find they don't really care about what you're saying, and if they do, they may display some competitiveness. To spot an egomaniac, look out for someone with extreme confidence. They will likely carry a sense of entitlement which manifests in an attitude of "This is so unfair!" over something minor. Egomaniacs are usually alone, but if they're not, they are accompanied by other egomaniacs or a very submissive partner.

*The real need*: Most times, what can appear as egomania is actually a deep insecurity and weak emotional foundation. Deep down inside, they feel there is something lacking so they must overpower this gut instinct by shouting about how great they are. If they don't do this, they will have to face their true feelings about themselves, and they are so weak, they cannot handle this reality. What they really need is recognition – but not about their surface accomplishments. Instead they need assurance about their deeper qualities. They have so much insecurity about their real self, that they overcompensate and show-off with the other aspects of their life they can control, such as what car they drive, who they've slept with, or how much money they make.

Sometimes, however, the egomaniac you've met is a sociopath. They do not feel remorse or empathy, and they can be extremely smart. These people do not crave recognition, and their need is simply to dominate others.

*Solution:* An egomaniac cannot take criticism well and is not capable of accountability, so you'd be wasting your time trying to get an apology. The best way to deal with them is to not take what they say seriously and avoid giving them the flattery that they desire. In discussions, only deal in facts and never emotions. Remember, they do not care about your emotions, only their own.

**2. The Bully**

No one likes a bully and if you encounter one, it's likely you're not the only person trying to fight him off. The bully enjoys shaming, humiliating, or singling out the people around him. He gets a noticeable thrill from catching someone off guard or seeing them speechless after he belittles them. Most of the time, a bully only acts this way when he's in group settings. One-on-one, you may find him to be quite insecure and standoffish, but not always. Adult bullies can cause just as much damage as child bullies, but unfortunately, they aren't confronted on their behavior as much; adults do not like admitting that they are dealing with a bully.

*The real need*: Bullies usually come from home lives where they were overpowered or bullied themselves. Their behavior is rooted in a feeling of having no control or power; this is why they seek out scenarios where they can feel powerful. Even if it's not rooted in a traumatic home life, the need of all bullies is similar: to feel powerful and superior by stirring someone's emotions and making them feel inferior.

*Solution:* Bullies enjoy inciting a reaction in their target, so whatever you do, act calm and avoid being reactive. Remain cool in the face of their aggression and they'll soon realize they can't get what they want from you. Realize that they are behaving from an immature, childlike need, so you must treat it as such. Do not give them the pleasure of feeling like they hold sway over your emotions. If you know this bully well, call them out on their behavior and do not let them get away with it.

### 3. The Victim

Make no mistake, the victim may look like a harmless, pathetic individual, but they can do a lot of damage, even without their realizing it. Victims always feel persecuted, like they're constantly getting the short end of the stick. They may accuse others of treating them differently or behaving cruelly towards them, even if no such thing occurred. These people love to talk about their personal problems. They are prone to oversharing and can do so for extended periods of time. If you try to bring up your own problems, they will respond with an attitude that says, "My problem is much worse." If a Victim causes harm to another individual, they have a hard time holding themselves accountable. They believe they cannot hurt others, since they are the real ones hurting.

*The real need*: At some point in the Victim's life, they did not get the empathy or sympathy they needed from an important person, such as a parent. During some life event, they were truly the victim in the situation but no one recognized this. Because they didn't get the closure they needed, they continued to carry this need for sympathy into the other areas of their life. The Victims are in need of empathy, but more than anything, they also need boundaries. They need to realize what happened to them in the past is separate from what's happening now.

*Solution:* To sidestep all the drama of the Victim, do not play into their hands. Once you get them started on their troubles, it's hard for them to stop. Instead, deal with them positively and give them the opposite of what they want to hear. Say things like, "I'm sorry to hear that, but it's great that at least you had wonderful friends to help you!" Even if they are not convinced by your positivity, it will show them they cannot drag you down into their self-pitying hole. If you know the person well, give them boundaries. For example, say you'll listen to them complain for five to ten minutes, but after that, you are only interested in discussing solutions to the problems.

### 4. The Negative Nancies

Like Victims, negative individuals can come across as nice people. Once you get into a more in depth conversation, however, you'll notice one thing: they exude so much negativity! They are distrustful and always see the downside of every issue. They will discourage you from the slightest risk, and you may leave interactions with them feeling more worried, and a lot less excited.

*The real need*: In the negative person's eyes, they are not being negative, only realistic. By being negative, they are attempting to gain control over the situation by staying aware of the worst case scenario. At some point in the past, they let their guard down and something bad happened that was out of their control. Ever since then, they've needed to feel like they have control, so they always expect the worst case scenario. Unfortunately, by doing this, it tends to become a self-fulfilling prophecy.

*Solution:* Counter their negativity with positivity, but remember that it's not your responsibility to make them happy. Show the Negative Nancy that they do have control over creating a positive outcome. And show them that infusing negativity into every situation can actually bring about a negative outcome. Consider sharing some interesting stories from your life where you took a risk and it resulted in something highly positive.

5. **The Contrarians**

It's normal to have a dose of contrarianism in us, but true contrarians take it to an extreme. It doesn't matter what you say, even if it's completely reasonable, the contrarian will always take the opposing side. They love to debate and don't really care what people think about them. Oftentimes, they'll even play Devil's advocate, taking on an unpopular opinion, just to spark a good argument. Anyone who loves debating may get along with a contrarian, but even then, the constant challenge can get exhausting.

*The real need*: The needs of contrarians can vary. Sometimes the individual really wants to come across as a unique person – someone who stands out of the crowd. Other times it can come from a genuine distrust of authority; so whatever the leading opinion is, they immediately expect something suspicious behind it. When they stand up against a perceived authority, it is a rebellion and an attempt to feel superior. Sometimes they feel they are doing the right thing, but other times it is purely to satisfy their own ego. If they can own you in an argument, then in their mind, they have asserted their superiority over some authority force.

*Solution:* Contrarians are some of the most likely personalities to start arguments. The best way to avoid it is to focus on finding common ground with them. Since they are so passionate about certain issues, a "let's agree to disagree" approach may not always work. In this case, try to take a listening approach. Instead of arguing, question them about their opinions and get them to explain it to you further. It cannot become an argument if you don't insert your opinion into the matter.

If you do argue with a contrarian, stick to the facts. Do not get noticeably frustrated or overcome with emotion as some contrarians enjoy this. Another way to avoid a debate is to get the contrarian to tell you their opinion first. That way you'll know how to agree with them and prevent an argument.

## When is it okay to lie?

We're all told that lying is bad, but it's not always that simple. We should never lie to manipulate or mislead, but there are many occasions where lying may be helpful or beneficial. If you're not sure whether it's okay to lie in a particular situation, ask yourself these questions. The more times you answer 'yes,' the more likely it is that you *shouldn't lie*.

- If I lie, will I prolong a situation that's harmful to someone?

- If I lie, am I enabling someone's unhealthy delusion?

- If I lie, will I save myself from potential danger?

- If I tell the truth, will I lower their self-esteem?

- If I tell the truth, will I hurt someone's feelings over something they have no control of?

# Job Interview Preparation

# Chapter 8 - Using Conversation to Get What You Want

The best conversationalists are constantly using words to wield their way. It can be something as minor as convincing a friend to come out with you or as major as convincing your boss you need a massive raise. And if you're not doing it, chances are it's been done to you. The craziest part is you're not going to even be aware of the most successful ploys against you. The most persuasive conversationalists can slip by unnoticed like a black cat in the dark.

As we've demonstrated, it's never just about what you say, it's also largely about how you behave. Your behavior will set the stage for your words, and will strongly influence how they come across. That's why, in the arena of persuasion, we must also begin with behavioral tactics.

## Subtle ways of showing dominance

Showing real dominance is not just about being a jerk or acting cocky. In fact, if you're coming across as a nasty person, you're just displaying aggressive behavior. This takes no skill and it's not a sustainable method of taking or maintaining power. You're playing on everyone's need to defend themselves against violence by cornering them, and making them feel they have no other choice. True dominance, on the other hand, is achieved by getting others to follow your lead willingly.

If two people, equal in experience and skill, are interviewed for the same job, dominant behavior can make one party appear more competent. Why? It's about far more than what you see on paper. A person who displays dominant behavior shows potential leadership abilities and the big winner, confidence. It presents the illusion that their competence is stronger than the other person, even if it may not be true. Even outside of the professional arena, dominant behavior makes it more likely for people to listen to you and it increases your level of attractiveness to the opposite sex.

That said, you don't need to become a total alpha to succeed, you just need to keep some of these tips in mind for when the right scenario reveals itself.

### 1. Make your body bigger

The psychology behind this sign of dominance has its roots in our animalistic natures. In the animal kingdom, many beasts display the largeness of their size in order to intimidate the other contenders. The one that appears biggest wins by default, without the need to incite violence. Humans can also do this to successfully assert their dominance. To make your body look big, open out your chest, stand tall, and if it doesn't look unnatural, put your hands on your hips. In addition to the above, women can also show dominance by wearing high heeled shoes.

### 2. Walk through the middle of the room

When in a crowded room, people have a tendency to make their body smaller and move through whatever side of the room has the most space. Instead of adjusting to the room, try making the room adjust to you. Walk through the middle of the room, even if there's a crowd, and expect people to move out of the way for you. Most people want to avoid bumping into someone, so they'll budge if you refuse to.

### 3. Sit at the head of the table

The person who sits at the head of the table oversees everything. They can keep a watchful eye on anyone, and they occupy the only seat that does not share its level with someone else. The next time you're with a group, sit in that dominant seat.

### 4. Use hand gestures and touch

To assert dominance, make good use of your hands. Make sure to initiate handshakes by extending your hand first. Then remember, to shake firmly. While you're talking, use your hands expressively, but keep your wrists strong and never limp. Dominant individuals also touch other people, even if they don't know them very well. This is not sexual. This can be a friendly knock on the shoulder, a slap on the knee, or perhaps even a hand placed on their back followed by a directive statement like, "Let's get you another drink."

### 5. Speak with a louder voice

Studies have shown that the loudest voice in the group is seen as the most dominant. Even if they speak less than others, it will make all others pause due to its volume alone. Use your lungs and diaphragm to achieve a louder voice. As you attempt this, do not yell or shout while you're in conversation, as this will only alarm and possibly scare away the people around you.

It is also extremely important to ensure that your voice never gets higher in pitch when you converse. When we are in the presence of someone we feel is superior, our voices immediately get higher pitched than usual. Keep your voice at its normal pitch at all times to avoid coming across as submissive.

Now that we've got our behavior under control, let's get a back-and-forth going.

## Persuasion Techniques for all Situations

### 1. Framing

When it comes to swaying people in a direction of your choice, the art of framing is a classic. When we frame something, we highlight whichever attributes will help our argument best, while paying less attention or even hiding its less appealing factors.

Let's say you're trying to convince a friend of yours to go on holiday with you and your family. To help your argument, you should mention the beautiful location, the fun activities, the luxurious hotel rooms, the attractive locals, etc. And you should avoid talking at length about your annoying Aunt Margaret and the fact that it'll be crowded during the tourist season. If your friend already suspects the risks, then acknowledge them, but emphasize the aspects that will help your argument.

### 2. The yes ladder

This psychological technique has proven successful at eliciting a 'yes' response when used correctly. The first step is to think of the big question you need a positive response to. Once you've determined what this is, start thinking of smaller, relevant asks that are more likely to get a 'yes' response. Gradually work your way through the easy asks, before ending with the big question.

For example, let's say you're trying to convince your family to go on holiday, but you know they're hesitant to leave their normal routine. You would start off with questions like, "Do you ever feel like there's so much in the world you haven't seen yet?" and "Do you agree that life is most fulfilling when you're taking risks and experiencing something new?" You could even throw in, "Do you ever feel like you're wasting your life playing it too safe?" Chances are they will say yes to all these questions. Once you've extracted all the 'yes' answers, your big ask has a much higher chance of success. Finally, you ask, "Perhaps it's time, then, to go on holiday and finally have some new experiences?"

### 3. The unreasonable request

If the yes ladder isn't quite your approach, then why not try the opposite? Instead of building yourself up to a big ask, start with an unreasonable ask. It's important to make sure, however, that you don't actually want this unreasonable ask. You're expecting the other person to say no to this so that when you finally get to your smaller request, it seems a lot more reasonable. For example, let's say you're asking someone to donate to your charity. Start off by saying, "Would you be interested in making a $200 donation?" When they shake their head and say no, you can finally say, "We understand. In that case, how about just a $10 donation?"

## 4. Emphasize the benefits

To effectively convince someone of a course of action, you must consider the benefits they'll experience. Never assume that people will do anything simply out of the kindness of their hearts, especially if you're not a close friend or relative. When you're trying to persuade someone, really emphasize the benefits they'll receive if they agree to what you're saying. This works across the board, for all situations. If there's a reason they're reluctant, show them how one of the benefits will help them solve that problem. If you're trying to convince a coworker to get lunch with you, but he's too busy making last minute touches on a project, don't just emphasize how great the food will be. Be specific to his benefits. For example, you could say that he'll probably work much more efficiently once he eats some good food.

## 5. Speed up or slow down your speech

A known persuasion rule is that if an audience is most likely to disagree with what you're saying, increase the rate at which you're speaking. We see this a lot in salesmen where they will talk faster so that the person they're speaking to becomes overwhelmed with information. This gives them less time to notice things that may be incorrect and they are less likely to form a counter-argument.

If you think the odds are in your favor, the opposite will be beneficial. Slow down your speech if you think there's a strong possibility that your audience will agree with you. This will ensure that others feel more satisfied about their decision. If you give them time to assess all the information you've presented, they will feel as though they came to the conclusion completely on their own. They won't feel as though they were subjected to persuasion tactics, and this will make them happier with their decision.

# Three Tricks to Seduce Someone through Conversation

First of all, let's get one thing straight. If someone has zero attraction towards you, this section can't turn those tables. In fact, you'll be hard pressed to find anything that can. It can, however, turn a little bit of attraction into a lot of attraction. If there's something there, it can be kicked up a notch with these tips.

**1. Fractionation**

Fractionation is a Neuro-Linguistic Programming tool and its original intentions were not for seduction. In fact, it was used to enhance a patient's state of hypnosis during hypnotherapy. Today, it is thought to be a controversial technique for seduction, but one thing is for sure: it works. It involves using a hot-then-cold dynamic where desire is elevated through intermittent reinforcement.

It is easy to use this seduction method in an unethical way, but we don't advise resorting to abusive behavior. Instead, consider the many ethical ways we can use fractionation to stir desire.

- Incorporate hot-then-cold conversation topics. During ordinary conversation, we tend to start with light-hearted conversation. And if we care to prolong the interaction, it often deepens until it is at its most intense state, and both parties experience some level of exhaustion. When we use fractionation, we go back and forth between topics of intensity and topics that are more casual. It's up to you which one you start with, but you should always make the transition natural. Go from casual jokes, to discussion about your families, to lighthearted banter about TV shows, to heartbreak, and so on.

  Make sure the serious topics bring your feelings into play, and the lighthearted topics should be factual or humorous. This rollercoaster of moods will intensify the feeling of intimacy. The other person will feel like they've shared everything with you, and you will earn their trust.

## Job Interview Preparation

- Make push and pull statements. When making statements that both push and pull a partner, it's important to keep both sides equal. Too much of a push, and they'll think you're a mean person or simply not interested. Too much of a pull, and they'll think you're needy and clingy. Push and pull statements allow you to express your feelings without overwhelming someone. When done right, they can pique interest and enhance desire.

To formulate the ideal statement for your situation, choose an aspect of their personality to compliment (don't make up a good quality - really choose one she embodies) and turn a conventional response on its head. For example, you could say, "I hate how amazing you are at guitar. It's such a blow to my ego." It's also important to deliver this line with humor and playfulness, so they perceive it as positive instead of negative. Another example of such a statement is, "You dress so well, I'm starting to think you shouldn't be seen with me." Whatever you choose to say, make sure it does not come across as an insult.

**2. Insinuation**

Quite simply, insinuation is the act of planting a thought or idea in someone's head. Instead of forcing a direction, you simply let this carefully-planted seed grow on its own. When we use insinuation to seduce, we allow the object of our desire a quick glimpse of what we have in mind.

- Touch a person briefly, especially when they aren't expecting it. We advise doing this on a part of the body that is bound to send a tingle up their spine, though one should stay far away from all private regions. Lay a hand on the lower area of the back, affectionately rub someone's shoulder or grasp gently just above the knee.
- Make the occasional seductive glance, especially while keeping conversation light-hearted. Use your eyes to

communicate how you truly feel, while your words stay in the safe zone.

- Use smart double entendres. The keyword here is 'smart.' Most people do not respond well to vulgar sexual innuendos, but a well-placed double entendre, at just the right time, can make a potential lover stir. It does not have to be sexual, it can be simply romantic. A double entendre is any statement that could have two meanings. If you're talking about your career, you could slip in the line, "I'm the kind of man who goes after what he wants and doesn't let go." This counts as a double entendre, since you could be talking about romantic pursuits as well. If you accompany this with an eye-gaze, you may just make the other person swoon. A sexual double entendre is a little riskier, but if you read the signals right, this could turn up the heat on your date.

### 3. Pauses

You know all about sexual tension, don't you? When we can't have someone exactly when we want them (and the feeling is mutual), our sense of desire grows and grows, until it's off-the-charts. As we've demonstrated, suspense enhances all emotion. And this is exactly why a well-timed and well-placed pause can be highly powerful. Here are some examples of when a pause can be effective.

- In a great compliment. Before you conclude the compliment, insert a pause that can be accompanied by eye-gazing or a shy smile. Let's say you're complimenting your current crush. You could say, "You look… stunning." This pause makes the compliment seem a lot more thoughtful and genuine, like you really thought about it, instead of just blurting it out.

- In a vulnerable statement. If you're discussing or explaining something in the realm of feelings, add a pause before the most revealing part of your sentence. This will add to the intimacy and vulnerability of the situation. If you're on a promising date, you could say, "I feel… like this is really going well." Pause. "Do you feel the same way?"

## Six Highly Effective Tips for Successful Negotiations

Negotiations most commonly happen with our employers or managers, but they are not restricted to the professional realm. When we're young, we may negotiate with our parents, and once we're older, we may negotiate with our partners. The sign of a successful negotiation is both parties walking away satisfied. Someone's goal is reached and the other side does not feel lesser for it. The other party may even feel it's for the best. To ensure your future negotiations are providing you and the people in your life with maximum benefits, keep these tips in mind.

### 1. Make timing your ally

Pay close attention to the frame of mind your negotiation will be met with. Timing can make all the difference between a successful deal and one that misses the mark. If you try to negotiate with someone who is rushing to another appointment, just heard bad news, or just finished a heated argument with another person, you are very likely not going to get the response you want.

### 2. Do not use submissive or weak language

When you find yourself in this situation with a superior, it may be tempting to use submissive language to soften your request. Before you begin negotiating, you may want to say "I hate to ask you this but…" or "I hope this isn't too much but…" so you don't come across as demanding. This can actually weaken your request. If the opposing negotiator has a streak of arrogance, they may even use your disclaimer against you and act more aggressive. Do not give them fodder to do that with. Be confident and assertive, knowing your full value. Avoid acting submissive but also steer clear of acting entitled. Find a balance between the two.

## 3. Share honest information

When you're in this situation, especially in a professional setting, it can be easy to feel like you should be guarded. This isn't true. Being honest with your employer or other authority figure can actually help your case. For example, if you need a raise because you feel you're not getting what you're worth, and perhaps you've started to struggle financially, this can give your boss more incentive to give you what you want.

## 4. Always have a first offer in mind

You're in a vulnerable position, so it's only natural to cringe at making the first offer. You may also think that it's wise to feel out the situation before any numbers are cast. Studies have shown, however, that those who make the first offer get closer to their goal. If you're looking for a raise, you're more likely to get your target salary if you have an offer in mind. This is because the first offer is what the negotiations revolve around. Instead of bending yourself to your employer's offer, they will bend themselves to yours. The first offer anchors the situation, so make sure it's yours.

## 5. Be brave with your offer

Make sure that your offer is not too low. People are often afraid to ask for too much, but studies have actually shown that you're more likely to low-ball yourself. Reflect on what your ideal outcome is and do not feel obligated to play it safe. Your ideal outcome may be more possible than you think!

## 6. Consider what they would gain from saying 'yes'

You can't walk into a room and just make demands. Unless the other party has something to gain from meeting your demands, you can kiss their cooperation goodbye. Before negotiating, consider the extent of their gain to figure out just how much you'll be able to ask for. This gain could be anything, from receiving better performance or improved efforts from you. Or perhaps the benefit is keeping you instead of losing you.

Don't shy away from using conversation to get what you want. The reality is: everyone is doing it. And guess what? You probably are too – just subconsciously. When we act subconsciously, our actions are not under our control, and anything could happen. Take control now and start getting the outcomes you desire.

# Conclusion

Congratulations on making it to the end of *Conversation Skills 2.0*! You should be proud of yourself and your newfound abilities. Social interactions can seem complex and overwhelming, but the new knowledge you've gleaned has placed you leagues ahead of the rest.

It's not that complicated once you break it down, is it? You'd do well to remember the big three rewards that we all look for in our human connections: safety, significance, and expansion. For the best outcomes, make your new acquaintances feel like they can trust you, like you appreciate them, and as though you have the ability to expand their horizons in some way, even if it's through humor and entertainment. Everything is grounded in these three major needs. Try and always satisfy them.

You've learned how to display likable behavior and give yourself an advantage for all proceeding conversations. In no time, you'll be brightening up a room and attracting connections like never before. You've also gained the tools for igniting interesting interactions, building magnetism, and developing deeper relationships with new and existing connections. And in addition to all of this, you've armored up for difficult social scenarios and learned persuasion techniques for a variety of social arenas.

Remember that it all begins with you. Learn to love yourself, stay true to who you are, and embrace your unique qualities. When we're comfortable with who we are, we let others in and we have more to offer them in our everyday conversations. Do what needs to be done to replenish your self-esteem and you'll easily stay a top-dog in your social interactions.

Another teaching I want you to take away is this: human beings are not as difficult as you think they are. Don't approach them with hesitation or fear. They are more similar to you than you realize, they've just accumulated different layers.

We can all be likened to locked treasure chests, filled with all manner of curious and fascinating things. Approach other humans the way you'd approach a locked treasure chest; take the time to find the right key and don't feel discouraged if one doesn't work. With patience, kindness, openness, and respect, try to experiment with different ways to open this box. What you find inside could be a great reward.

Human beings are social animals, so when we master conversation skills, connections are amplified and self-satisfaction becomes the new norm. Isn't that a reality you'd like to see?